Herodotus

Swayne

Ancient Classics for English Readers

EDITED BY THE

REV. W. LUCAS COLLINS, M.A.

HERODOTUS

The Volumes published of this Series contain

HOMER: THE ILIAD, BY THE EDITOR.

HOMER: THE ODYSSEY, BY THE SAME.

HERODOTUS, BY GEORGE C. SWAYNE, M.A.

CÆSAR, BY ANTHONY TROLLOPE.

VIRGIL, BY THE EDITOR.

HORACE, BY THEODORE MARTIN.

ÆSCHYLUS, BY REGINALD S. COPLESTON, B.A.

The following Authors, by various Contributors, are in preparation :—

XENOPHON.
SOPHOCLES.
EURIPIDES.
ARISTOPHANES.
CICERO.
JUVENAL.
HESIOD.
PLINY'S LETTERS.

OTHERS WILL FOLLOW.

A Volume will be published Quarterly, price 2s. 6d.

HERODOTUS

BY

GEORGE C. SWAYNE, M.A.
LATE FELLOW OF CORPUS CHRISTI COLLEGE, OXFORD

WILLIAM BLACKWOOD AND SONS
EDINBURGH AND LONDON
MDCCCLXX

c. W. H

M.

CONTENTS.

INTRODUCTION.

So little is known for certain regarding the life of Herodotus, "the father of history," that it may well be a subject of congratulation that he has not shared the fate of Homer, the father of poetry, in having doubt thrown on his individual existence.

He appears to have been born about the year 484 before Christ, between the two great Persian invasions of Greece, at Halicarnassus, a colony of Dorian Greeks on the coast of Asia Minor. His family was one of some distinction. From his writings alone we should know that he received a liberal education, and became familiarly acquainted with the current literature of his day; and the epic form of his great prose work, besides numberless expressions and allusions, bears witness to the fact that the Homeric poems were his constant study and model.

His early manhood was spent in extensive travels, in which he accumulated the miscellaneous materials of his narrative. He visited, in the course of them, a great part of the then known world; from Babylon and Susa in the east, to the coast of Italy in the west; and from the mouths of the Dnieper and the Danube in the north, to the cataracts of Upper Egypt southwards. Thus his travels covered a distance of thirty-one degrees of longitude from east to west, and twenty-four of latitude from north to south—an area of something like 1700 miles square. It was an immense range in days when there were few facilities for locomotion, and when every country was supposed to be at war with its neighbours, unless bound by express treaties of peace and alliance. He travelled, too, it must be remembered, in an age when robbers by land and sea were members of a recognised profession,—very lucrative and not entirely disreputable : when (as we shall see hereafter) disappointed political or military adventurers took to piracy as a last resort, without any sort of compunction. " Pray, friends, are you pirates,—or what?" is the question which old Nestor puts to his visitors, in the 'Odyssey,' without the least intention either of jesting or of giving offence. A voyage itself was such a perilous matter, that a Greek seaman never, if he could help it, lost sight of land in the daytime, or remained on board his ship during the night; and at a later date the philosopher Aristotle distinctly admits that even his ideal "brave" man may, without prejudice to his character, fear the being drowned at sea. The range of our author's travels is, however, less wonderful than their busy minuteness. He is traveller, archæologist, natural philosopher, and historian combined in one. He appears scarcely ever to have concluded his visit to a country without exhausting every available source of information. Personal inquiry alone seems to have satisfied him, wherever it could be made ; though he consulted carefully all written materials within his reach, records public and private, sacred and secular. He rightly calls his work a "History," for the Greek word "history" means really "investigation," though it has passed into a different use with us. In Egypt alone he seems to have spent many years, visiting and exploring its most remarkable cities—Memphis, Hieropolis, and the "hundred-gated" Thebes. In Greece proper, as well as its colonies on the Asiatic seaboard and in South Italy, and in all the islands of the Archipelago, he is everywhere at home, as well as in the remoter regions of Asia Minor.

Such details of his life as have come down to us rest on somewhat doubtful authority. It is said that he was driven from Halicarnassus to Samos by the tyranny of Lygdamis, grandson of that Queen Artemisia whose conduct he nevertheless, with some generosity, immortalises in his account of the battle of Salamis ; that in Samos he learned the Ionic dialect in which his history is written ; that in time he returned to head a successful insurrection against Lygdamis, but then, finding himself unpopular, joined in the Athenian colonisation of Thurium, in Italy, where he died and was buried, and where his tomb in the market-place was long shown. His residence at Samos may have been a fiction invented to explain the dialect in which he wrote, which was more probably that consecrated by usage to historical composition. At one time he appears to have removed to Athens, where he received great honours, partly in the substantial shape of ten talents (more than £2400), after a public recitation of his history. According to one story, he was commissioned to read it before the Assembly of all the Greek States on the occasion of

the great national games held every fourth year at
Olympia in Elis.

Amongst the audience on some such occasion, most
probably at Athens, a young Athenian, Thucydides,
is said to have been present; and the introduction
which then took place may have given the first
stimulus to the future historian of the Peloponnesian
war, who, despairing of surpassing his predecessor as
a charming story-teller, boldly struck out for himself
a new path, as the founder of the critical method. It
seems also that at Athens Herodotus enjoyed the friendship of the great tragic poet Sophocles. Plutarch has
preserved the opening words of a poem in which the
tragedian compliments the historian, after he had quit-
ted Athens for Thurium. In two of the tragedies of
Sophocles, the 'Œdipus at Colonos' and the 'Antigone,'
are passages plainly adapted from this history. The
society of Athens under Pericles, comprising all that
was most select and brilliant in art and intellect, must
have had great attractions for Herodotus; and it im-
plies some self-denial on his part to have torn himself away from it. Probably he longed to exercise,
as most Greeks did, full political rights, which, as an
alien, he could not enjoy at Athens, though he was
evidently an enthusiastic admirer of her institutions.

After his emigration to Thurium, he seems to have
devoted his life to the elaboration and amplification of
his great work. Several passages in his history prove
that he was, at all events, acquainted with the earlier
events of the great Peloponnesian war. The balance
of evidence seems to point to his death having occurred
when he was about sixty. If so, he at least escaped
witnessing, as the result of that war, the fall of his

beloved Athens from her well-won supremacy over Greece.

The history of Herodotus is a great prose epic, suggested doubtless to the author in early life by the fame of those events which were still fresh in the minds of all men—the repulse of the Persian invasion, and the liberation of Greece. The Greeks had thrown off colonies, from time to time, into the islands of the Levant and the west coast of Asia.* These Asiatic Greeks had actually been enslaved by Persia; and European Greece, though free from the first, could only wake to the full consciousness of that freedom when the overshadowing dread of the monster Asiatic power had been dissipated. Independence could be but a name for either Athenian or Spartan, so long as the very sight of the Persian dress (as Herodotus tells us) inspired terror. Until Miltiades won Marathon, by a rush as apparently desperate as our Balaklava charge, the Persians had been reputed invincible. Their second expedition against Greece was intended to repair the damaged prestige of Persian valour, by setting in motion overwhelming numbers. It seemed as if the dead weight alone of Asiatic fleets and armies must carry all before it. It did indeed carry Athens, but not the Athenians. The sea-fight of Salamis was won by citizens who had lost their city. The two great victories which followed within a year—Platæa and Mycale, gained on the same day—indicated for ever the superiority of Europeans over Asiatics. The latter was fought out

---

* Of these colonies, some were Ionian, some Dorian, and some Æolian, having been originally founded by each of these old Greek races. But Herodotus usually speaks of them all as "Ionians," as these took the most active share in the war.

on Asiatic ground—the beginning of the great retribu-
tion which has continued even to the present time,
represented by uncertain tides of Western conquest
gradually gaining ground on the East.

Never before or since has an author employed himself with grander subject-matter than Herodotus. The
victories of Freedom in all ages, more than any other
conquests, have stirred the human heart to its depths.
It is the cause that alone humanises war, and makes it
other than brutal butchery. Many such victories there
have been in the course of time, but all of local and
limited importance in comparison. And, indeed, perhaps Marathon made Morgarten possible. By Salamis
and Platæa the world may have escaped being oriental-
ised for ever, and bound in the immobility of China.
These battles, by saving freedom and securing progress,
anticipated the overthrow of the Saracens before Tours,
and of the Turks before Vienna. Herodotus, indeed,
could not see all this, when the plan of his great history dawned on his mind, but the salvation of his beloved Greece was to him a sufficient inspiration.

We find the same unity of design in the history of
Herodotus as in Homer's great epic. As in the 'Iliad,'
not the siege of Troy but the wrath of Achilles is the
continual burden, so, in our author's work, not the history of Greece but the destruction of the great Persian
armada is its one great subject. All the other local
histories, though introduced with much fulness of
detail, are subordinate to this consummation. They
flow to it like the tributaries of a river, whose might
and grandeur make men love to explore its sources.
He gives us in succession the early history of Lydia,
of Babylon, and of Assyria, in order to trace the rise

and fall of those several Asiatic powers which merged
at last in the great empire of the Medes and Persians,
who are the actors in his true drama, to which these
preliminary histories are a discursive prologue. His
work is not a romance founded on fact, like Xenophon's 'Education of Cyrus,' or Shakspeare's historical plays, or Scott's 'Quentin Durward.' It is
serious history, as history was understood in his time.
But the historian's appetite was omnivorous in the
collection of materials, and robustly digested fable and
fact alike. His mind was like that of Froissart and
Philip de Comines, who lived in another age, when
miracles were thought matters of course. Yet in Herodotus we perceive the dawning of that criticism
which finds its full expression in Thucydides, who was
in mind a modern historian, though less fastidious as to
the evidence of facts than a man of our century would
be. The incredulity of Herodotus, when it shows itself,
seems rather evoked by the suspected veracity of his
informant, or some contradiction in phenomena, than
by the incredible nature of the facts themselves.

He has been most found fault with for ascribing
effects to inadequate causes ; but we ought rather to feel
grateful to him, considering the mould in which the
mind of his time was cast, for endeavouring to trace
the connection between cause and effect at all. In
Homer the gods are always in requisition, and always
at hand to manage matters, even in minutest details.
That Herodotus had a religious mind there can be no
doubt, for he speaks even of foreign and barbaric
rites and beliefs with intense respect. And the great
Liberation War of Greece was, in its circumstances, cal-
culated to illustrate one great pervading principle of his

religion—that heaven will not allow an excess of
mortal prosperity. The rock which overhung the bay
of Salamis, whence Xerxes looked down on his
host, might well bear the statue of Nemesis. Nemesis,
in the religious system of the ancient Greeks, is
the great divine stewardess, who assigns to man his
quota of good or of evil. If man takes to himself more
good than his share, she adjusts the balance by giving
him evil; for the gods are jealous of those who try to
vie with them. Did not Apollo flay Marsyas for daring
to contend with him on the lyre? Did not Minerva
change Arachne into a spider for boasting to be a better
spinster than herself? So the Sovereign of the gods
cannot endure the luxury and pride of the earthly
despot. It becomes the business of Nemesis to com-
pass his destruction. She invokes against him Atè,
or Infatuation. Atè blindfolds his mind, and forces
him to enter of his own will on the path whose end is
destruction. To ward off this, men resort to sacrifice;
but any sacrifice short of what is most precious is useless. Polycrates, the despot of Samos, almost insults
the gods in supposing that throwing a jewel into the
sea will atone for the crime of prosperous sovereignty;
the ring comes back to him in a fish brought to his
table. Was not Agamemnon compelled to sacrifice
his daughter, the pride of his house, before he could
obtain a fair wind to sail to Troy? It seems to have
been an article of the Athenians' creed, which Herodotus shared, that there was a sort of wickedness in
one free man attempting to rise above the level of his
fellow-citizens; and perhaps they thought that their
honourable punishment of ostracism was devised as

much for a great man's good as for theirs.* It was a
kind of inverted doctrine of the divine right of kings,
traces of which we find throughout the Attic literature.
Had Herodotus lived in our day, we may imagine
that his attention would have been powerfully arrested
by the fate of Napoleon the First, or the Czar Nicholas
of Russia, as illustrating this sentiment.

Frequent references will be found in these pages to
Mr Rawlinson's 'History of Herodotus;' but it is
desired here to acknowledge more distinctly the use
which has been made of his exhaustive volumes.

The History of Herodotus was divided by the ancients into nine books, each bearing the name of one
of the Muses. His own order of narration is very discursive, for he digresses into local history and anecdote
continually. In these pages a rearrangement into
chapters will perhaps be more welcome to the general
reader.

* Ostracism was so called from the oyster-shells on which
Athenian citizens wrote their names in voting. Any man of
more than average greatness or goodness was liable to incur
this left-handed compliment, which consisted in his being requested to go abroad for a term of years, in case a sufficient
number of votes was given. It was instituted as a security to
democracy, and as preventive of *coups d'état*. It was dis-
credited at last by its application to the case of a vulgar dema-
gogue. The Syracusans had a similar institution called "Petal-
ism," from the leaves of olive on which the names were written.

THE HISTORY OF HERODOTUS.

CHAPTER I.

CRŒSUS.

> " And ever, against eating cares,
> Lap me in soft Lydian airs."
> --MILTON, " L'Allegro."

In the great quarrel between Europe and Asia, which is the end and scope of our author's work, it is of the utmost consequence to the satisfaction of his religious principles that the balance of blame should incline to the side of the true offenders. According to the showing of the Persians themselves, who had their story-tellers, if not historians, the Asiatics were the first offenders. A Phœnician skipper went to Argos, and carried off Io, the king's daughter, to Egypt, whither he was bound. By way of reprisals, the Greeks then carried off two women for one—Europa from Tyre, and Medea from Colchis. This may have partly excused Alexander or Paris, son of Priam king of Troy, for carrying off Helen, the wife of Menelaus, from Sparta, in the second generation afterwards. But then, said the Persians, the Greeks put themselves clearly in the wrong

—for instead of carrying off another lady, they made the abduction of Helen a case of war. " To carry off women was manifestly the deed of unjust men, but to make so serious matter of their abduction was the part of simpletons, since they hardly could have been carried off without their own consent." Indeed, according to one account, Io at least eloped of her own free will. But in fact, our historian thinks, from the time of the Trojan war the Asiatics looked upon the Greeks as their natural enemies.

Without discussing too curiously all these tales, Herodotus has no doubt in his own mind that the blame ought to lie with the Asiatics, since Crœsus, king of Lydia, was the first historical aggressor. Before his time all the Greeks were free, and he was the first Asiatic potentate who, by fair means or foul, reduced Grecian states to various kinds of dependency. The towns on the coast he subdued by force, easily enough. He had proposed to try the same means with the islanders of the Archipelago, when he was dissuaded from his purpose by a shrewd jest. Among other travellers who visited his court was one of the Seven Wise Men of Greece—Bias of Priene. The king asked him, as he did all his visitors, what was the last news? "The islanders," said Bias, "are busy raising a force of cavalry with which they mean to invade Lydia." Crœsus declared it was the very thing he could wish,—but he hardly believed they could be so utterly foolish. Bias ventured to think that the Greek islanders would be equally amused to hear that the Lydians intended to attack them on their own element. The king took the hint: and it is the earliest specimen we have of the wisdom which after-

wards so often clothed itself in the language of the
" Court Fool."

The Lydians appear to have been a people, like the
Egyptians, of nearly immemorial civilisation, and, like
the Asiatic tribes who fought for the Trojans, to have
had a common origin with the Greeks themselves, and
to have differed little from them in manners and customs.   There is manifest truth in the tradition which
connected them with the Etruscans and the Pelasgians;
and their three dynasties, of the second of which Hercules was said to be the founder, may have represented
three cognate races of conquerors, like the Saxons,
Danes, and Normans with us.   They appear to have
been at first a warlike people, but to have been ener-
vated by conquest, and then, like the descendants of
the ancient Italians, to have become chiefly famous as
artists, especially as musicians.

This Crœsus, the son of Alyattes, in time extended
his empire over most of the countries westward of the
river Halys.   He was, in some sort, the Solomon of his
age; fabulously rich, magnificent in his expenditure,
and of unbounded hospitality; so that great men came to
visit him from all parts, and to gaze on the splendours
of his court.   Amongst them was Solon the Athenian.
Solon had remodelled the laws of Athens, with the
concurrence of the Athenian people ; but, knowing the
fickleness of his countrymen, had gone into voluntary
exile for ten years, having bound them by oath that
they would make no change in their institutions in his
absence.   Crœsus, in the course of his conversations
with Solon, wished to extract from him the confession
that he considered him the happiest of mankind.
Solon refused to account any man happy till death had

set its seal on his felicity, and took occasion to warn
Crœsus of the instability of all human affairs, dilat-
ing especially on the jealous nature of the gods. The
king could not brook the plain-speaking of his guest,
and dismissed him in disfavour. He was soon to
prove the truth of his warning: the terrible Nemesis,
says our author, was awakened—probably, he thinks,
by this very boast of thinking himself the happiest of
mortals. Then he goes on to tell, in his own delightful
fashion—

The Story of Adrastus.

Crœsus had two sons—the one grievously afflicted, for
he was deaf and dumb, but the other by far the first
of the youths of his age, by name Atys. Now Crœsus
dreamed that he should lose this Atys by the stroke of
an iron weapon. Through fear of this dream, he took
him no longer with him to the wars, but sought out
for him a wife who might keep him at home. Nay,
he even had all the weapons that hung in the men's
rooms stacked away in the inner chambers, lest any of
them might fall on him by accident. While the marriage was preparing, there came to seek refuge at Sardis
a Phrygian of royal birth who had committed homi-
cide. Crœsus purified him with the due rites, and
then inquired his name. He said, "I am Adrastus,
son of Gordias; I slew my brother by misadventure,
and my father has turned me out of doors, and I have
lost all." And Crœsus answered, "Thou art the son
of a friend, and art come to friends; with me thou
shalt lack nothing. Thou wilt do best to bear thy
mishap as lightly as thou mayest." About this time
it came to pass that a huge wild boar came out of

Mount Olympus in Mysia and laid waste the fields; and the people came to Crœsus and besought him to send to them his son to help them with the hunting-train. And Crœsus, mindful of the dream, refused to send his son, but promised to send the train and picked sportsmen of the Lydians. But his son Atys coming in, was much vexed, and said, "Thou bringest me to shame, my father, in the eyes of the citizens and of my bride, in that thou dost forbid me to go to the wars and the chase, as though I were a coward." But Crœsus said, "I hold thee no coward, yet I do wisely, for I was warned by a dream that an iron weapon should slay thee; therefore did I give thee a wife to keep thee at home. For thou art in truth my only son, for the other I count as though he were not, being deaf and dumb." Then answered the son, "It is natural, my father, to take good heed on my behalf, after such a dream. But what iron weapon hath a boar, or what hands to hurl it? If indeed thou hadst dreamed that I should die by a tusk, thou wouldst be wise in doing what thou doest, but not now, for this war is not with men." Crœsus confessed himself persuaded by these words, and allowed his son to join the chase; but he begged Adrastus to go with him and guard him, lest any evil should happen by the way; and Adrastus, though heavy of heart, deemed that he could deny Crœsus nothing in return for his kindness, and went accordingly. So the hunters made a great hunt, and having brought the boar to bay, stood round and threw javelins at him. And it came to pass that Adrastus threw his javelin, and missed the boar, and killed the son of Crœsus. So the dream was fulfilled. Now Crœsus, when he heard the news, was

sorely troubled, and in his anguish called on Jupiter as
lord of purification, as lord of the hearth, as lord of
companionship, to witness what he suffered at the
hands of his suppliant, his guest, and the man whom
he had sent to guard his son.   And now came the
Lydians bearing the corpse, and behind them followed
the slayer, Adrastus.   And he, standing before the
bier and stretching forth his hands, besought Crœsus
to take his life, as he was no longer worthy to live.
Then Crœsus, though in great grief, pitied him and
said, "Thou hast made full atonement, in that thou
hast judged thyself worthy of death.   Thou art not
to blame, but as a tool in the hands of some god, who
long since did signify to me what should come to
pass." So Crœsus buried his son, and spared Adrastus.
But when he was departed, Adrastus, as thinking himself of all men the most wretched, slew himself upon
the tomb.   And Crœsus mourned for his son for the
space of two years.   But at the end of that time he was
fain to bestir himself, for there came to him a rumour
that Cyrus the Persian had conquered the Medes, and
was exalting himself above all the kings of the earth ;
and he hasted, if it were possible, to crush the Persian
power before it became too strong.

———

Crœsus, in Herodotus' story, appears in close relations with the god Apollo.   The world-famous shrine of
this god was at Delphi on Mount Parnassus, currently
believed to be the exact centre of the earth—the earth
itself being looked upon as a round disc.   In the temple
there, the site of which was supposed to be the spot
where the serpent Python was slain by the arrows of
the Sun-god, there was an oracle, the most renowned

in the world. Its answers, in spite of their ambiguity, guided the public and private affairs of the Greeks to an extent which appears to us now almost ludicrous. Though generally vague and perplexing, yet they were often so much to the point, that some of the old Fathers of the Church attributed them to Satanic influence, as they doubtless would table-turning and spirit-rapping, if they lived now. It was also believed that their efficacy ceased exactly with the coming of our Lord, by which time, at all events, faith in them had worn out. Milton alludes to this tradition in his " Hymn on the Nativity ":—

" The oracles are dumb ;
  No voice or hideous hum
    Runs through the archèd roof in words deceiving.
  Apollo from his shrine
  Can no more divine,
    With hollow shriek the steep of Delphos leaving.
  No nightly trance, or breathèd spell,
  Inspires the pale-eyed priest from the prophetic cell."

Before he determined on his expedition against Cyrus, Crœsus sent to test the most famous oracles in Greece and that of Jupiter Ammon in Libya, in order that he might know which was most to be trusted. And he made the trial thus : he told his messengers to ask each oracle, on the hundredth day after their departure, what Crœsus was doing at that particular hour. The other answers are unrecorded, but the answer of the priestess of Apollo at Delphi ran thus :—

" Truly the tale of the sand I know, and the measures of
    ocean—
Deftly the dumb I read, I list to the voice of the silent,

A. C. vol. iii.   B

Savour has reached my sense from afar of a strong-
skinned tortoise
Simmering, mixed together with flesh of lamb, in a caldron;
Brazen the bed is beneath, and brazen the coverlet over."

Crœsus, when he received this answer, judged the god
of Delphi to be the wisest, since he alone could tell
exactly what he was doing—for he had been cooking the
flesh of a tortoise, mixed with lamb's flesh, in a brass
caldron with a brass lid. Accordingly he sent rich
presents to the shrine of Apollo, and ordered all his subjects to pay him especial honours. Thus having satisfied himself that this oracle at least was true, he next
sent to inquire if he should go to war with the Persians. The answer was, that if he did so "he would
ruin a great empire;" at which answer Crœsus rejoiced
greatly, for he expected to destroy the empire of the
Persians. He sent a third time and inquired of the
oracle if his reign would be long? And the oracle
answered :—

"When it shall come to pass that the Medes have a mule
for monarch,
Lydian, tender of foot, then along by the pebbles of
Hermus
Flee, and delay not then, nor shame thee to quail as a
coward."

Crœsus rejoiced still more when he heard this, for he
thought that, as a mule could never reign over men,
the rule of himself and his descendants would never
come to an end.

His next step, still under the advice of the oracle,
was to make friends of the most powerful Greek
states. At this point Herodotus, having wound his
readers up to the expectation of a catastrophe, like some

modern novelists, diverges into one of his favourite
episodes, and takes advantage of the fact that Crœsus
found the leading Greek states to be the Lacedæmonians and Athenians, to relate a part of their history.

At Athens, Pisistratus, the son of Hippocrates, had
now raised himself to absolute power. Athens being divided between the parties of the Plain and the Coast, he
had headed the third, called the party of the Mountain,
and by pretending that his enemies had wounded him,
managed to be allowed a body-guard, and then seized on
the citadel. He had some vicissitudes of fortune before
he was firm in the saddle, and on one occasion returned
to Athens in a chariot accompanied by a woman of
great beauty and stature, who personated the goddess
Athenè (Minerva).* The success of the imposition is
possible, if we remember that the early Greeks believed that the gods sometimes came down visibly
among mortals. By whatever devices, however, he
gained or secured the sovereignty, he appears to
have ruled well and righteously, and to have done
much for the civilisation and glory of Athens.

The Spartans or Lacedæmonians were now beginning
to assert the leadership which they afterwards obtained in the Peloponnese, as a consequence of those
laws of Lycurgus, whose sole end and object was to
make Sparta a model barrack for a state of soldiers.

With the Spartans Crœsus had no difficulty in concluding an alliance, as the path of friendship had

---

* If he had also been accompanied by the owl of that goddess,
the case would have been very like one which occurred in the
remembrance of this generation, when a fugitive prince landed
in France with a tame eagle on his shoulder.

been paved by a previous interchange of gifts and civilities; they had also heard of the Delphic prophecies. He immediately proceeded to commence a campaign against the Persians by marching into Cappadocia. A sensible Lydian made one last effort to dissuade him. "O king," said he, "thou art about to march against men who have trousers of leather, and all the rest of their dress of leather, and they feed not on what they would like but on what they have; for their land is rough. Nay more, they are unacquainted with wine, being water-drinkers, and they have no figs to eat, nor anything else that is good. If thou conquerest them, thou canst get nothing from them, for they have nothing to lose; if thou dost not, thou wilt lose all thine own good things. There will be no thrusting them back when once they have had a taste of what we enjoy; nay, I thank the gods that they do not put it into the mind of the Persians to march against the Lydians."

In undertaking this war, Crœsus was prompted partly by ambition, partly by his desire to punish Cyrus for dethroning Astyages, the king of Media, who was his brother-in-law. Crossing the river Halys,* the northern boundary, he advanced to the country near Sinope, on the Black Sea—in modern times notorious as the scene of the destruction of the Turkish fleet by the Russians. Here Cyrus marched out to meet him. A battle took place in which both sides claimed the victory. Crœsus, however, thinking his numbers too small for ultimate success, determined to fall back on Sardis, and begin the war again after the winter with larger forces. He sent round to his allies to tell them to join him in four

* Now the Kizil Irmak.

months' time. But his long course of prosperity was
drawing to its close. Cyrus had not been so crippled
by the battle but that he could march straight to Sardis and so "bring the news of his own arrival." Crœsus, though surprised, led out the Lydians to meet him.
They were at this time as good men of war as any in
Asia. They fought, like the knights of chivalry, on
horseback, with long lances ; and the plain before Sardis was the battle-field of their predilection. But Cyrus
invented a device to paralyse this cavalry. Taking
advantage of a horse's natural fear of camels, he or-
ganised a camel brigade and placed it in his front, with
infantry behind it, and his own cavalry in the rear.
Though the Lydian knights, like the Austrians at Sem-
pach, dismounted and fought on foot, the battle went
against them, and Crœsus soon found himself besieged
in his capital. Then he sent messengers to his allies
urging them to help him with all speed.

The Spartans, even had they been able to reach
Sardis in time, could not set out at once, as they happened just then to have their hands full. They
were fighting with the men of Argos about a tract
of borderland called Thyrea. Argos had been in the
old Homeric times the head of the Peloponnesus,
and was always very jealous of Spartan supremacy.
The plausible plan had been adopted of fighting out
this particular quarrel by three hundred chosen men
on each side ; though three on each side, as in the
affair of the Horatii and Curiatii between Rome and
Alba, might have answered the purpose quite as well.
The combat proved as deadly as that between the
rival Highland clans recorded by Scott in his 'Fair
Maid of Perth.' Two only of the Argives were left,

who ran home with the news of the victory; while a single Spartan, raising himself up from amongst a heap of dead, remained in possession of the field and set up a trophy. So the result was considered indecisive, and the main armies fell to fighting, and the Spartans conquered. Then the Argives shore their hair, which they formerly wore long, and bound themselves under a curse not to let it grow again till they had recovered Thyrea, and forbade their women to wear gold ornaments—a prohibition probably more difficult to enforce. The Spartans, in retaliation, made a contrary vow, to let their hair grow, having worn it cropped before. The survivor of their three hundred was said to have slain himself for shame.

In the mean time Crœsus was a lost man. The citadel of Sardis had been scaled by the Persians at a point where a king of old had omitted to carry round a lion, which was to operate as a charm to prevent its being taken. It has been mentioned that Crœsus had a son who was deaf and dumb. His father had tried in vain all means to cure him of his affliction, and given up the attempt in despair. But now, when Sardis was taken, a soldier approached Crœsus, not knowing who he was, to slay him; and Crœsus, in his deep grief, did not care to hinder him, which he might have done by giving his name, since Cyrus had issued express orders to his army that the king of Lydia was to be taken alive. Then suddenly the tongue of the youth was loosed, and when he saw the Persian approaching, he cried out—" Fellow, do not kill Crœsus!" and having made this beginning, he continued able to speak for the rest of his life. Thus Crœsus was taken prisoner, after a reign of fourteen years, and Cyrus, in the cruel spirit of

the age, placed him on a pile of wood, with the intention of burning him alive. Then Crœsus bethought
him of the wise words of Solon, how no man should be
accounted happy until the end, and in his anguish
called aloud thrice upon Solon's name. Cyrus asked the
meaning of the cry, and when he heard the story, was
so touched that he ordered the pile, which was already
lighted, to be put out. But this could not be done
by all their exertions until Crœsus prayed to Apollo for
aid, when suddenly a great storm of rain came on and
extinguished the fire.

Cyrus treated his royal prisoner with all honour.
When the Persian soldiers began to plunder Sardis,
Crœsus inquired of his conqueror what they were doing.
" Spoiling thy goods, O Crœsus." " Nay, not mine,"
replied the fallen monarch, "but thine, O Cyrus."
Then Cyrus stopped the sack of the city, and in grati-
tude for the suggestion of Crœsus, begged him to name
any favour he could do him. " My lord," said he,
" suffer me to send these chains to the god at Delphi,
and to ask if this is how he requites his benefactors,
and whether ingratitude is an attribute of Greek gods in
general ? " For Crœsus had loaded the shrine of Apollo
with costly presents. The message was sent, and the
priestess of the oracle made this reply : " Crœsus atones
for his forefather Gyges, who slew Candaules his master. Apollo desired that the judgment should fall on
the son of Crœsus and not on himself, but the gods
themselves cannot avert fate. The god did what he
could, for he deferred the fall of Sardis three years
beyond the destined time : secondly, he put out the
fire, and prevented Crœsus being burnt alive : thirdly,
he did not give a lying oracle, for he only said that

Crœsus should destroy a great empire, without saying what empire it should be. Crœsus had no right to interpret his words according to his own wish. As to the oracle about the mule, he might have known that Cyrus was a Persian by his father's side and a Mede by his mother's, and so a hybrid king." Crœsus was obliged to acquiesce in the explanation, and to take his fate patiently. His ruin was, indeed, no common bankruptcy. "As rich as Crœsus" soon grew into a vernacular proverb. Yet he was by no means a bad specimen of the millionaire. His gentleness and good-nature were as proverbial as his wealth, and Pindar, the Theban poet, testifies to this point—doubtless for substantial reasons of his own :—

> "Of kindly Crœsus and his worth
> The name doth never fade."

The strange vicissitudes of his life became a fertile subject for Greek romancers and moralists. His riches seem to have been derived partly from the grains of gold brought down in the sand of the river Pactolus, which made Asia Minor the California of antiquity. This was doubtless the origin of the fable of the Phrygian king Midas turning all that he touched to gold. It seems that Sardis in early times was an important place of trade, as Herodotus says that the Lydians were the first coiners of money and the first storekeepers, so far as was known. It was at the same time notorious as the great slave-market of the world.

CHAPTER II.

CYRUS.

> " Not vainly did the early Persian make
> His altar the high places, and the peak
> Of earth-o'ergazing mountains, and thus take
> A fit and unwalled temple, there to seek
> The Spirit, in whose honour shrines are weak
> Upreared of human hands."
>
> —BYRON, " Childe Harold."

BEFORE the Medes or Persians made their appearance
in history, the Assyrians, according to Herodotus, had
ruled over upper Asia for five hundred and twenty
years. Asshur appears in Scripture * as a son of Shem,
who went out from the land of Shinar and founded
Nineveh. Herodotus is supposed to have written a separate history of Assyria, which has been lost ; but Layard
and others have deciphered for us a new history from
the monuments of that wonderful empire. The bearded
kings and warriors, with their wars and lion-hunts
graven on sandstone slabs, which are to be seen in the
British Museum and in the Louvre in Paris, look as
fresh as if they had been sculptured yesterday instead
of nearly three thousand years ago. The Assyrians
were of the Semitic race, of the same family as the

* Gen. x. 11, 22.

Jews and Arabs; while the Medes and Persians were, in Scriptural phrase, of the sons of Japheth—that is, they belonged to the same Aryan, Iranian, or Indo-Germanic family as the Greeks and Romans, and ourselves. The home of the Assyrians and their cognate Babylonians was in the great plain of Mesopotamia, while the Medes lived in the mountains to the east, and the Persians to the south-east. The Median highlanders, being of more hardy habits, first conquered the Assyrian lowlanders, and then, descending to their softer country and habits, were conquered in their turn by the hardier Persians. The decline of Assyria was consummated by the fall of Nineveh, which was taken, about B.C. 625, by Cyaxares, third king of the Medes, in conjunction with the Babylonians. The first king of the Medes is said to have been Deioces, who built the wonderful city called by Herodotus Agbatana,* and less correctly by later writers Ecbatana, with its seven circular walls, one within the other, with the palace and treasuries in the centre. The first wall had white battlements, the second black, the third scarlet, the fourth blue, the fifth orange. The last two walls had their battlements silvered and gilt. They rose one above another on a conical hill, and were supposed to have had a symbolic meaning, as referring to the sun, moon, and five planets, or the deities presiding over the days of the week. The last king of the Medes was Astyages, the son of Cyaxares. He had given his daughter Mandane in marriage to Cambyses, who was, according to our author's account, a poor Persian gentleman, but according to later authorities, a descendant of the first Persian king Achæ-

* In the Behistun inscription it is Hagmatâna.

menes. Astyages dreamed that he saw a vine spring from the body of his daughter Mandane, which overshadowed the whole. of Asia. We know from Scripture how much stress the Chaldeans and the Medes laid on dreams. Fearing that an offspring of Mandane would deprive him of his sovereignty, Astyages ordered the son that was born of her to be destroyed. The courtier Harpagus, who was commissioned to do this, passed on the child to one of the royal herdsmen, that he might expose it to die upon the mountains. But the herdsman's wife, when she saw that it was "a proper child," and plainly of noble birth, adorned for death with gorgeous apparel, took pity on the infant, and as she had just lost one of her own, persuaded her husband to expose the dead child, and save the living one, that she might nurse it. So the future Cyrus lived, while the herdsman's child received a royal funeral. When the boy was ten years old he was playing one day with the children of his village. The game was King and Courtiers. Cyrus was chosen king, and assumed the dignity as if he had been born to it, appointing officers, architects, guards, couriers, and an official called the King's Eye,* (possibly the head of the detective police).

* This officer is introduced in Aristophanes' comedy of 'The Acharnians.' He appears in a mask (as in a modern burlesque) with a single huge eye in the centre. He is brought to Athens by some envoys who have been at the court of Persia. Dicæopolis (an honest farmer who is present at the reception) is indignant at their waste of time and the public money.

"*Envoy.*—We've brought you here a nobleman—Sham-artabas
　　　By name, by rank and office the King's Eye.
Dicæop.—God send a crow to peck it out, say I!
　　　And yours th' ambassadors' into the bargain."
　　　　　　　　　　　—FRERE'S Transl.

In carrying out his character, Cyrus ordered one of the children, the son of a Median of high rank, to be flogged for disobedience. The angry child went to the city and complained to his father, who in turn complained to the real king. Astyages ordered the despotic urchin to be brought into his presence. Unabashed, however, the boy justified himself; and this circumstance, together with a strong family resemblance, led to his recognition by the grandfather, who came at the truth by examining the herdsman and Harpagus. He now dissembled his wrath, pretended that he was glad the child had been saved, and invited Harpagus to send his son to be the companion of the young prince, and to come himself to dinner. After Harpagus had well feasted, Astyages asked him how he liked his entertainment; he said it was excellent. Upon this, a basket was shown to him containing the head, hands, and feet of his own son, on whose flesh he had been feasting. The father, with the dissimulation natural to the subjects of an Oriental despotism, observed that whatsoever the king did was right in his eyes. It is the very answer which the son of Ethelwold is said by William of Malmesbury to have made when King Edgar showed him his father's corpse, slain by him in the royal forest; the English chronicler having evidently borrowed from Herodotus.

Astyages now consulted the Magi (a caste of priests of whom we shall hear more hereafter) as to what was to be done. They said that they considered that Cyrus had ceased to be dangerous, since he had been king already in the children's play. So Astyages sent him away into Persia, to his real parents. Meanwhile

Harpagus nursed his revenge, till Cyrus was grown to man's estate, and then he felt his time was come. He sent a letter to the noble youth sewn up in the belly of a hare, bidding him put himself at once at the head of the Persians, and revolt from Astyages. This king —surely under some infatuation from heaven, says the historian—forgetting the deadly wrong which he had done Harpagus, sent him to suppress the revolt. He deserted to Cyrus, and the Medes were easily defeated. Thus Cyrus destroyed the great Median empire, and substituted that of the Persians—becoming, after the downfall of Crœsus, master of all Asia. He treated his grandfather Astyages with all honour to the day of his death.

There was a religious as well as a political dissidence between the two nations. They both worshipped the elements and "all the host of heaven," and planetary deities ; but the Persian national creed recognised both a good and an evil principle in nature, constantly at war, whom they called Ormuzd and Ahriman. The Persians, according to Herodotus, eschewed images, temples, and altars, and sacrificed to the elemental deity on the tops of mountains. But he has evidently confused the Median worship with theirs. Their habits much resembled those of the old Germans, as described by Tacitus. They were originally a simple people, and compulsory education with them was limited to teaching their sons " to ride, to draw the bow, and speak the truth." Next after lying, they counted running in debt most disgraceful, since "he who is in debt must needs lie." Lepers were banished from society, as they were supposed to have sinned against the sun ; even white pigeons being put under "taboo" for a similar reason.* They were very much given to wine ;† and discussed every subject of importance twice—first when they were drunk, and again when they were sober. As water was a sacred element, none might defile a river—a sanitary regulation in which we moderns would do well to follow them. The bodies of the dead presented a difficulty. They might not· be buried, for the earth was sacred; or thrown into rivers, for water was sacred ; or burnt, for fire was sacred. They were therefore exposed to be torn by birds and beasts—a fate of which the Greeks had the greatest horror. The Parsees of India, and the native Australians, dispose of their dead in much the same way. As a compromise, adopted from the Magi, a body might be buried when covered with wax to prevent its contact with the earth.

The Persians, when they had conquered the Medes, soon degenerated from their earlier simplicity, which is celebrated by Xenophon in his romance of the 'Education of Cyrus.'

When Cyrus, by the defeat of Crœsus, had made himself master of Lydia, the Greek colonists on the Asiatic seaboard sent to him in alarm, and begged to be allowed to be his vassals on the same terms as they had been to Crœsus. He answered them by a scornful parable : " There was a certain piper who piped on the

---

* So to this day, in India, all *white* animals are looked upon much in the way in which we ourselves regard albinoes—a kind of unhealthy *lusus naturæ.*

† Their successors retain the taste. "It is quite appalling," says Sir H. Rawlinson, "to see the quantity of liquor which some of these topers habitually consume, and they usually prefer spirits to wine."

sea-shore for the fish to come out, but they came not. Then he took a net and hauled out a great draught of them. The fish, in their agonies, began to caper. But he said, ' Cease to dance now, since ye would not dance when I piped to you.'"* This answer drove the Ionian Greeks to fortify their towns and send ambassadors to Sparta for assistance. Their envoy, however, disgusted the Spartans by wearing a purple robe and making a long speech—two things which they detested ; and they voted not to send the succours, but despatched a fifty-oared ship to watch the proceedings of Cyrus. When this vessel reached the port of Phocæa, a herald was sent on to Sardis to warn Cyrus from the Spartans not to hurt any Greek city on pain of their displeasure. This caused Cyrus to inquire who these Spartans were, and how many in numbers, that they dared to send him such a message. When he was informed he said, " I am not afraid of people who have a place in their city where they meet to cheat each other and forswear themselves " (meaning the agora or market-place); " and if I live, the Spartans shall have troubles enough of their own, without troubling themselves about the Ionians."

Cyrus had other business on his hands at present than to punish the Greeks ; he therefore went back to Ecbatana, leaving a strong garrison in Sardis. But while he was on his way he heard that one Pactyas had induced the Sardians to revolt, and was besieging the garrison in the citadel. Troops were sent to put down the revolt; Pactyas, however, did not wait for their arrival, but fled to Cyme, on which the Persian general demanded his extradition. The men of Cyme sent to

* This Eastern apologue may serve as an illustration of the parable in Matt. xi. 16.

ask advice at a neighbouring oracle of Apollo, and the
answer came that Pactyas was to be given up. Some
of the citizens, not satisfied with this answer, thought
the envoys must have made a mistake, and sent again
to remonstrate with the god, but the answer was
repeated ; whereupon Aristodicus, the principal envoy,
went round the temple and cleared away all the
nests of sparrows and other birds that he found there.
While he was thus engaged, a voice came from the
sanctuary,—" Unholy man, darest thou to tear my suppliants from my temple ?" on which Aristodicus, by no
means abashed, replied,—" O king, thou canst protect
thine own suppliants, and yet thou orderest the Cym-
æans to surrender theirs." " I do," answered the god,
"that you may the sooner perish ; for it was in the
naughtiness of your hearts that you came to consult me
on such a matter."* Eventually they sent Pactyas to
Chios for safety ; but the Chians gave him up to the
Persians, even tearing him from the temple of Minerva ;
and Atarneus, a district opposite Lesbos, was paid them
as the price of blood. But there was a curse on the
produce of Atarneus for ever.

The Persians now proceeded to punish the revolted
Lydians and Ionians, and Harpagus, the king-maker,
who had deposed Astyages, forthwith beleaguered
Phocæa. The inhabitants of this city, however, preferred exile to slavery ; taking an oath never to

* The remarkable answer attributed here to the oracle may
serve to illustrate the permission given to Balaam to go with the
messengers of Balak. Even to the heathen mind, there were
questions of conscience so clear, that to consult heaven specially
in the matter was a mockery. [See the almost parallel case of
Glaucus, ch. viii.]

return until a bar of iron, which they sank in the sea, should rise and float, they set sail, and, after a multitude of adventures, found a resting-place on the coast of Italy.

Most of the other towns on the coast were subdued after a gallant resistance, and the islanders gave themselves up. Then Harpagus turned inland against the Carians and Lycians. The Carians deserve notice as the reputed inventors of crests to helmets, and of heraldic devices. The Lycians were early advocates of the rights of women; naming men not after their fathers, as was usual, but after their mothers. The Lycians of Xanthus * made a desperate resistance. Finding they could not beat the Persians in the field, they made a great pile on which they burnt their wives and children, and all their valuables, and then sallied out and perished in battle to a man. Their example was imitated by Saguntum in Spain in the second Punic war.

While Harpagus was thus subduing the coast, Cyrus was pursuing his conquests in Upper Asia. He turned his arms against Labynetus, king of Babylon. This renowned city, says our historian, formed a vast square fifty-five miles in circuit. Its double walls were 340 feet high (nearly as high as St Vincent's rock at Bristol) and 85 feet thick. The measurements seem enormous, yet the great wall of China shows such works to be possible, when absolute power commands unlimited labour. The city itself was cut in two by the river Euphrates, the quays being fenced by walls with

* About thirty years ago the British Museum was enriched by some beautiful marbles brought from Xanthus by an expedition which explored Lycia under the conduct of Sir Charles Fellowes.

water-gates for communication. One half contained
the king's palace, the other the great sacred tower of
Belus (Bel or Baal) with its external winding ascent.
Babylon was in fact a fortified province rather than
a city; it resembled Jeddo in Japan, in being a collection of country houses with small farms and gardens
attached. It seems to have been the ideal of what a
great city ought to be, especially in days of internal
railroads. London, containing its millions, with its
thin houses laterally squeezed together, or Paris, with
its horizontal piles of flats, and no corresponding
spaces, would have excited the horror of the ancients, who in some respects were more civilised than
ourselves. Herodotus attributes the great engineering
works about Babylon, to prevent the Euphrates from
overflowing the country, chiefly to two queens, Semira-
mis* and Nitocris, between whom he places an interval
of five generations. Of this latter he relates a striking
anecdote.

"She built for herself a tomb above the most fre-
quented gateway of the city, exactly over the gates,
and engraved on it the following inscription: 'If any
of the kings of Babylon who come after me shall be in
need of money, let him open my tomb and take there-
from as much as he will; but unless he is in need, let
him not open it, else will it be worse for him.' Now
this tomb remained undisturbed until the kingdom fell
to Darius. But he thought it absurd that this gateway
should be made no use of—for it was not used, because
one would have had to pass under the dead body as one

---

* This queen appears to have really reigned in conjunction
with her husband. She is probably not the great queen known
by the same name.

went out—and that when money was lying there idle,
and calling out for some one to take it, he should not
lay his hand on it. So he opened the tomb and found
no money at all, but only the dead body, and these
words written—' If thou wert not the greediest of men,
and shameless in thy greed, thou wouldst not have
disturbed the resting-place of the dead.' "

Although the author notices most of the wonders of
Babylon, he makes no mention of the hanging-gardens,
which excited the astonishment of later writers. Nebuchadnezzar is said to have constructed them out of affec-
tion for a Median wife, that she might not be afflicted
with a Swiss longing for her native mountain scenery.*

Having defeated the Babylonians in battle, Cyrus
drove them inside their huge walls. There they
laughed at his efforts, having good store of provisions
for many years. But their enemy proved himself as
good an engineer as any of their queens, historical or
fabulous. Taking advantage of reservoirs previously
existing, he turned off by a canal the waters of the
Euphrates, and the Persians walked into the city dry-
shod by the bed of the river, even the water-gates
having been left open by incomprehensible carelessness. Those who were in the centre of the city, says
Herodotus, were still feasting, dancing, and revelling,
after the Persians had entered. It is the night described in the Book of Daniel, when the terrible
" handwriting" was seen upon the wall.†

The Babylonians were a luxurious people. Their

---

* So a great fox-hunter, who could not find it in his heart to
leave England, is said to have turned his conservatory into a
little Italy for his delicate wife.

† The names of the Eastern kings are so· variously given,

full dress was a long linen tunic, with a woollen robe over it, and a short white cloak or cape over the shoulder. Though they wore their hair long, they swathed their heads in turbans, and perfumed themselves all over. Each citizen carried his walking-staff, carved at the top with the likeness of some natural object—such as an apple, a rose, a lily, or an eagle—and had also his private signet. Of these seals (which are hollow cylinders) great numbers have been found during the late explorations, and brought to Europe.*

Herodotus records one of their customs, which, whether in jest or earnest, he declares to be the wisest he ever heard of. This was their wife-auction, by which they managed to find husbands for all their young women. The greatest beauty was put up first, and knocked down to the highest bidder; then the next in the order of comeliness—and so on to the damsel who was equidistant between beauty and plainness, who was given away gratis. Then the least plain was put up, and knocked down to the gallant who would marry her for the smallest consideration,—and so on till even the plainest was got rid of to some cynical worthy who decidedly

that it is almost impossible to identify them either in sacred or profane history. The Labynetus of Herodotus is Nabonidus, or Nabonadius, in other writers. The "Belshazzar" whom Daniel calls "king" was probably his son, associated with him in the government. His name appears in inscriptions as Bilshar-uzur. We know from other authorities that Labynetus himself was not in the city at its capture.—See Rawlinson's Herodotus, i. 524, &c.

* They are commonly of some composition, but occasionally have been found in amethyst, cornelian, agate, &c.—Layard's Nineveh and Babylon, 602, &c.

preferred lucre to looks. By transferring to the scale of the ill-favoured the prices paid for the fair, beauty was made to endow ugliness, and the rich man's taste was the poor man's gain. The Babylonian marriage-market might perhaps be advantageously adopted in some modern countries where marriage is still made a commercial matter. It at least possesses the merit of honesty and openness, and tends to a fair distribution of the gifts of fortune.

Another Babylonian custom, of which Herodotus strongly approves, was that of employing no professional physicians, but placing the sick in the gate of the city, that they might get advice respecting the treatment of their diseases from every passer-by, and thus profit by the experience of those who had been afflicted in the same way as themselves. Whatever may be thought of the absence of regular practitioners, the alternative would certainly seem one of the exceptional cases where wisdom is not found in a multitude of counsellors.

Having annexed this great and rich province to his dominions, Cyrus seems to have been intoxicated with success, or, in our author's view, to have filled up the measure of his prosperity, which now began to run over in insolent self-confidence. He made an expedition against the Massagetæ or Greater Goths, who lived in the steppes near the Caspian Sea, and were ruled by an Amazonian widow named Tomyris. While encamping against her, Cyrus dreamed that Darius, the son of Hystaspes, a young noble of the royal house of Persia, appeared to him with wings on his shoulders (like some of the Assyrian gods whose figures he must have seen), with one of which he overshadowed

Asia and the other Europe. This portended his fall, and the ultimate accession of Darius. At first he gained a partial advantage by the stratagem of leaving a camp stored with wine to be plundered by the water-drinking Massagetæ, and then returning and massacring them in their sleep. This was the shrewd advice of Crœsus the Lydian, whom Cyrus had taken with him on the expedition. Among the prisoners taken was the son of the Massagetan queen. Cyrus released him from his bonds at his own request; but the youth, unable to bear his disgrace, only took advantage of his liberty to kill himself. At length the invaders were forced to a general action—the fiercest, says Herodotus, ever fought between barbarian armies. The Persians were completely defeated, and Cyrus himself was slain, after a reign of twenty-nine years. Queen Tomyris, exasperated by the treacherous slaughter of her army and the death of her son, had threatened to give the bloodthirsty invader his fill of blood; she kept her word by filling a skin with it, and plunging into it his severed head.

Such is the account which Herodotus gives of the death of the great Eastern conqueror, so famous both in sacred and profane history. He confesses that he has only chosen one legend out of many. There is little doubt, however, that he died in battle. But the Persian poets assigned a very different fate to their national hero, Kai Khusru, as his name stands in their language. They will not allow that he died at all. When he grew old, they say, he one day took leave of his attendants on the banks of a pleasant stream, and was seen no more. But, as in the case of Arthur and Barbarossa, and all the great favourites of a nation, they looked forward to his coming again, more power-ful and glorious than ever.

These Massagetæ, says our author, resembled the Scythians, but could fight on foot as well as on horseback, their favourite weapon being, as with the Anglo - Saxons, a battle - axe or bill. They had the peculiar custom of sacrificing their old people, and then feasting on them, and natural death was con-sidered a misfortune. This curious people, whose descendants may be now in northern or western Eu-rope, knew nothing of tillage, and lived on flesh, fish, and milk. Their only deity, known to Herodotus, was the Sun. To him they sacrificed the horse, with the notion that it was right to bestow the swiftest of creatures on the swiftest of gods. The Persians also attached a certain sanctity to some breeds of horses, and the Teutonic conquerors of Britain bore a horse as their cognisance. Some say that Hengist and Horsa were not names of men, but only represented a people using this national symbol. This rude heraldry of our northern ancestors—or conquerors—may still be traced in the "White Horse" cut out on the chalk-hills in more than one place on our Berkshire and Wiltshire downs.

CHAPTER III.

"In the afternoon they came unto a land
In which it seemed always afternoon."
—TENNYSON, " Lotos-Eaters."

OF all the nine books of Herodotus, the second, which
bears the name of the Muse " Euterpe," is incomparably
the one of deepest interest to the modern reader, as
giving glimpses, such as are found nowhere else but in
Scripture, of the infancy of the human race, and as
propounding important scientific problems, which can,
if ever, only find their solution in remote futurity.
It is, moreover, the portion of his work which is most
strongly stamped with the characteristics of the author's
personality. It must ever be borne in mind that Herodotus is not a historian in the modern sense of the term.
He is the representative writer of a class who stand mid-
way between poetical annalists like Homer and critical
historians like Thucydides. They wrote their Iliads
in prose, making no sharp distinction between truth
and fiction. They did not yet look upon the verifica-
tion of their facts as a duty, but jotted down all that
they heard and saw, an instinctive love of truth alone
suggesting occasional scepticism as to very extraordinary

marvels, so that the modern reader may just observe
the dawning of the critical spirit. Predominantly in
his Egypt, Herodotus appears as the traveller and
archæologist; nor is he fairly afloat on the current of
history until he launches himself into the narrative of
the Persian invasions of Greece, of the circumstances
of which he had more immediate knowledge—if not
as an eyewitness, yet from those who had themselves
been eyewitnesses.

Egypt has been in all ages the land of wonders,
from the time when its "magicians" found their en-
chantments fail before the mightier Power which was
with Moses, to that when Napoleon told his soldiers
that from the top of the Pyramids four thousand
years looked down on their struggle with the Mamelukes,—and to our own day, when a French engineer
repeats the feat of the old native kings and the Greek
Ptolemies, in marrying by a canal the Red Sea to
the Mediterranean; an achievement which will make
the name of Lesseps immortal, if the canal can only
be kept clear of sand. The civilisation of Egypt is
older than time—or at least, than its records. Her
kings were counted wholesale—not by individuals, but
by dynasties, of which there were said to have been
thirty-one, exclusive of gods and heroes. She was
the mother of the arts to Greece, as Greece has been
to us. Her monuments are nearly as vast and as
seemingly indestructible as the everlasting hills themselves, and the study of her mere remnants seems to
present a field as inexhaustible as that of nature. No
wonder that Herodotus willingly lingered in this interesting country. He was no holiday traveller, but
one all ears and eyes, not likely to let any fact or

object escape him through carelessness or want of curiosity.

The Egyptians were wont to boast that they were the oldest people in the world; but our author says that their king Psammetichus once put this to the proof, and decided against them. Two infants were kept carefully apart from human society, their attendants being forbidden to utter a word before them. Under these circumstances women as nurses were out of the question, and they were suckled by goats. [There was indeed a Greek version of the legend, which said that the children were nursed by women—with their tongues cut out.] One day, when about two years old, they came to their keeper, stretching out their hands, and calling "Bekkos! bekkos!" This being Phrygian for "bread," the palm of antiquity was adjudged to the Phrygians. The test was scarcely trustworthy, for probably enough the cry was only an imitation of the bleat of the goats. It has indeed been claimed by etymologists as the Sanscrit root "*pac*," whence our word "cook" is said to be derived. The Germans, again, recognise in it their own "bakken" = bake.*

According to the priests, who were Herodotus's chief informants, the whole country except the district of Thebes, seven days' sail up the Nile from the sea, was originally a swamp. To the truth of this our author was ready to testify, as the whole Delta (called so from the shape of the Greek letter Δ, our D) appeared to him to be "the gift of the river." This formation certainly required time, but he considered that the Nile was so

---

* Englishmen have suggested that it may have been a feeble attempt to call for "breakfast."

energetic, that in ten thousand years (which is, after
all, a very moderate geological period) it might even
deposit alluvial soil enough to fill up the Arabian gulf
of the Red Sea. The priests appear to have given
him very good data for supplementing his own obser-
vations on the physical phenomena of the country; and
in these details he evinces a patient investigation of facts
which would do credit to any age, however scientific.
He only becomes fanciful when he begins to speculate
on the unknown. With respect to the causes of the
annual inundations of the Nile, he could, naturally
enough, get no trustworthy information. It struck him
as particularly strange that the Nile, unlike other rivers,
should begin to rise with the summer solstice, and
be in a state of flood for a hundred days afterwards.
Certain Greeks who affected a reputation for science
endeavoured to account for the phenomenon in three
ways. The third, which appeared to Herodotus the least
plausible explanation, was, that the Nile was swollen by
melting snows, though it flows through the torrid land
of the Ethiopians into Egypt—which seemed to him a
contradiction. Yet this theory was so near the actual
truth, that the inundations are caused by the summer
rains in the highlands of Abyssinia and on the equa-
torial table-land of Africa. That Herodotus had seen
an inundation of the river is tolerably certain, from his
description of the appearance of the country at such
times. He speaks of the towns and villages standing
out of the water " like the islands in the Ægean Sea ;"
a graphic picture, of which modern travellers have
recognised the truth. Adopting neither of the theories
which had been advanced, Herodotus modestly propounds one of his own, which is curious, but of no

scientific value, as resting on false cosmographical
data.

As to the sources of the Nile, he says that he never
met with but one person who professed to know
anything about them. This was the registrar of the
treasury of Minerva at Saïs; but when he began to
talk about two conical hills—"called Krophi and
Mophi"—between Syene and Elephantinè (below the
cataracts), Herodotus thought he could hardly be
quite serious. Between those hills, said his informant, lay the fountains of the Nile, of unfathom-
able depth. Half the water ran to Egypt, the other
half to Ethiopia. Psammetichus had tried to sound
them with a rope many thousand fathoms in length,
but there were such strong eddies in the water that
the bottom of the spring could never be reached.
Herodotus himself went up the Nile as far as Elephantinè—that is, did not get beyond the first cata-
ract; and though he learnt much by inquiry as to the
country generally, he could throw no additional light
on the great question. But a story reached him
originally derived from certain Nasamonians—a people
inhabiting the edge of the desert—that once on a time
certain "wild young men," sons of their chiefs, took
it into their heads to draw lots which of them
should go and explore the desert of Libya, and try to
get farther than any one had gone before. Five of
their number set out, well supplied with food and
water, and passed first through the inhabited region,
then through a country tenanted only by wild beasts,
and then entered the desert, taking a direction from
east to west. After proceeding for many days over
a sandy waste, they came at last to a plain where

they found fruit-trees, and began to pluck the fruit.
While they were doing so, certain very small men
came upon them and took them prisoners. The Nasamonians could not understand them, nor make
themselves understood. They were led by them
across vast marshes, and at last came to a town where
all the inhabitants were black dwarfs like their captors. A great river flowed by the town from west to
east, abounding in crocodiles. And all the people in
the town were wizards. It was added that the ex-
plorers returned in safety from their perilous journey.
If the Bushmen now surviving at the Cape, and
formerly more extensively spread over Africa, were a
black race, which they are not, we might suppose
them to be the descendants of the little men spoken
of by Herodotus. Their colour may, however, have
been modified by the temperate climate of South Africa
in the course of long ages. The tribe of Dokos, in
the south-west of Abyssinia, are dwarfish, and answer
very nearly to Herodotus's description. Herodotus was
inclined to identify the Nile with the river flowing by
the mysterious city.*

It is strange that the oldest geographical problem in
the world should be a problem still, though now probably in the course of solution. The nearest approach
to the truth appears to have been made by the Alex-
andrian geographer, Ptolemy, who had heard of certain lakes as the sources of the Nile, and placed them
some ten degrees south of the equator. The question
slumbered through the middle ages, and one affluent
after another was looked upon as the true Nile, till

* It was more probably, as Mr Rawlinson and Mr Blakesley
both think, the Niger, and the city may have been Timbuctoo.

Bruce was for some time supposed to have set the question at rest in the eighteenth century, by the discovery of the source of the Blue River. Quite of late years it was agreed again that the White River was the main branch; and in 1857 Captain Speke, setting out from Zanzibar, discovered the Victoria Lake, which is now the farthest authenticated source in an easterly direction, while Sir Samuel Baker's Albert Lake is the farthest authenticated source in a westerly. Up to this time Speke and his companion Major Grant are the only men who have actually crossed Africa from south-east to north, and as yet the honours of discovery must be supposed to rest with them.

In treating of the wonders of Egypt, Herodotus certainly exaggerates on some points from love of paradox, as when he says that as the Nile differs from all other rivers in its nature, so the Egyptians differ from all other men in their habits, the men doing what is usually considered as women's work, and the women men's work; for in this he is refuted by the Egyptian paintings, which represent each sex as usually engaged in its proper occupation. But a Greek must have been much struck with the comparative freedom of the Egyptian women, so unlike the life of the Hellenic "lady's bower," or the Asiatic harem. Sophocles, in his ' Œdipus at Colonus,' has made a beautiful application of this recorded contrast to the helpful piety of the daughters and the selfish luxury of the sons of the blind hero, which would seem to show that he wrote the play fresh from the perusal of his friend's Egypt.

Our author makes the observation that the Egyptians were the first nation who, holding the soul to be immor-

tal, asserted its migration after death through the whole
round of created beings, till it lived again in another man,
which occupied a cycle of three thousand years. This
doctrine of a "circle of necessity" was held alike by
Buddhists, Druids, and—if Josephus may be trusted
—by the sect of the Pharisees among the Jews. But
this Egyptian doctrine, which is profusely illustrated
on the tombs, suffered the wicked only to descend into
animals, while the good passed at once into a state of happiness. A striking custom which Herodotus describes
would seem to show that to them, as to the Greeks,
the future existence was not a cheering prospect.

"In the social banquets of the rich, as soon as the
feast is ended, a man carries round a wooden figure of
a corpse in its coffin, graven and painted so as to re-
semble the reality as nearly as possible, from one to
two cubits long. And as he shows it to each of the
guests, he says, "Look on this, and drink, and be
merry; for when thou art dead, such shalt thou be."

The "skeleton at the banquet" has pointed many
a moral for ancient and modern writers. St Paul may
have had it in mind when he quoted as the motto of
the Sadducee, "Let us eat and drink, for to-morrow
we die," as well as Shakespeare, when he makes his
Hamlet moralise over Yorick's skull—"Now get you
to my lady's chamber, and tell her, let her paint an
inch thick, to this favour she must come."

Herodotus considers that the names of the gods
came to Greece from Egypt, with the exception of
Poseidon (Neptune), Castor and Pollux, Here (Juno),
Hestia, Themis, the Graces and the Nereids. All
these the Greeks were said to have inherited from the
Pelasgians, with the exception of the sea-god Posei-

don, with whom they became acquainted through the Libyans. The Egyptians, unlike the Greeks, paid no honour to heroes or demigods; for their god Osiris (who corresponded to Bacchus) appeared on earth only as a manifestation or Avatar of Deity. `Amongst the mythological marvels of the Egyptians, Herodotus relates that they accounted cows as sacred to Isis, the moon-goddess, represented with horns, and objected to kill them as food—a practice which finds its parallel in India at the present day. The sacredness of animals generally, in Egypt, struck our traveller forcibly. For each species there were certain appointed guardians, who tended and fed them, and the office was hereditary. To kill one of these sacred animals was a capital offence, unless done accidentally, in which case a fine was inflicted; but to kill an ibis or a hawk was death without reprieve. Cats were so much respected that, in case of a fire occurring, the Egyptians would let the house be burnt before their eyes, all their attention being given to saving the cats; which, however, they usually found impossible, as the animals (no doubt in terror at the well-meant efforts of their friends) had a trick of jumping into the flames. If they died, nevertheless, it was thought to be a terrible misfortune. When a cat died a natural death, all the inmates of a house went into mourning by shaving their eyebrows, and they shaved their heads and their whole bodies when a dog died. The dead cats were embalmed, and their mummies stored in the sacred city of Bubastis; but the dogs were buried in their own cities, as were also the ichneumons. The hawks and shrew-mice were conveyed to Buto, and the ibises to Hermopolis. It would seem by this that the animals about whose

funerals so much trouble was taken were more sacred
than the rest.* The crocodile, of which Herodotus
gives a description, perhaps as fairly accurate as could
be expected from an ordinary observer, was accounted
sacred by some of the Egyptians; for instance, by the
people about Thebes, and those about Lake Mœris.
In each of these places a tame crocodile was kept, who
wore ear-rings (or rather rings in the corresponding
holes) of glass or gold, and bracelets on his fore-paws.
Every day he had his ration of bread and meat, and
when he died he was buried in a consecrated vault.
But the people of Elephantinè, so far from canonising
these animals, thought them tolerable eating.

Herodotus gives a native receipt for catching crocodiles. Bait a hook with a chine of pork, and let it
float to about the middle of the stream. Let a confed-
erate hold a living pig on the bank, and belabour him
lustily. The crocodile hears the pig squeak, and, making for him, encounters the pork, which he swallows.
When the men on shore have drawn him to land, plug
his eyes with mud; after that, it is very easy to kill
him. This latter item of the receipt has a strong
affinity to an old precept about "putting salt on a
bird's tail." A very similar mode of capture (with this
exception) is practised by the natives now. The name
"crocodilos," as the author observes, is Ionic Greek
for "lizard;" the Egyptians themselves calling the
animal "champsa." † He is somewhat mistaken in his

* Lane says that the modern Egyptians are remarkably kind
to animals. On one occasion a lady buried a favourite dog
with all the honours due to a good Mussulman, and houseless
cats are fed at the expense of the Cadi of the district.

† Apparently an attempt to write the name *msah*, still to be

account of the hippopotamus, no specimen of which he appears to have seen. He gives it the hoof of an ox, and the mane and neigh of a horse.

The sacred bird called the phœnix Herodotus confesses he never saw except in pictures. Indeed it was rare in Egypt, for it came but once in five hundred years, when the old phœnix died. According to the pictures, it was like an eagle, with plumage partly red and partly golden. The bird was said to come from Arabia, bringing the body of his father enclosed in a ball of myrrh, that he might bury it in the temple of the Sun. Our author did not seem to be acquainted with that other version of the phœnix fable, according to which it returned from the east after a stated period to burn itself in frankincense, and was again resuscitated. The phœnix was an emblem of the soul and its supposed migrations, and its journey to the east typified the constant aspiration of the soul towards the sun. Its period of migration referred to a solar cycle in the Egyptian calendar. Pliny says that the name was derived from a species of palm in Lower Egypt, which dies down to the root and then is renovated. Ovid makes the bird build its nest on a palm. In hieroglyphic language the palm-bough is the sign of the year.

Amongst other wonders, our author had heard of winged serpents, which flew across from Arabia, and was induced to undertake a journey to the country whence they came, where he says he saw some of their bones. The ibises were said to destroy them as they flew, which caused this bird to be held in great honour by the Egyptians. We are now in possession of the

traced in the Arabic *temsah*.—See Sir G. Wilkinson's note, Rawlinson, ii. 116.

probable key to this enigmatical story, which illustrates
both the simple faith and painstaking of our author,
and also the manner in which myths grow out of the
use of words. When scorpions or snakes appear in
large numbers in the houses in Upper Egypt, they are
supposed to be brought by the wind, and to all such
objects an Arabic word is applied which signifies to
fly. Herodotus doubtless saw pictures of a winged serpent attacked by the ibis, but this bird typified the
god Osiris in the white robes of his purity, and the
winged serpent probably the Evil principle. The ibis,
however, is said to destroy snakes. His mention of
the harmless horned snakes at Thebes, which were
considered sacred, and buried in the temple, may suggest
the prolific subject of primeval serpent-worship.

The description which Herodotus gives of the manners and customs of the Egyptians stamps them as
a highly civilised people. In the reverence paid by
young men to their elders, he considered that they
set a good example to the Greeks. In the medical
profession they recognised a minute division of labour,
some being oculists, others dentists, and so forth.*
Those who embalmed the dead (the "physicians"
of the book of Genesis) formed a profession of themselves. He describes at length three methods of em-
balming (they had really many more), which were
adopted in order to suit the means of their customers,
as modern undertakers provide for funerals at different
tariffs. Amongst other local peculiarities, Herodotus
notices the lotus-eaters of the marsh-lands, who re-
mind us of those described by Homer in the voyage of

* "O virgin, daughter of Egypt, in vain shalt thou use
many medicines."—Jer. xlvi. 11.

Ulysses. But these latter—if they are to be identified at all—are to be recognised rather in the lotus-eating tribe whom our author mentions in a subsequent book as existing on the coast of Africa. Their lotus was probably a kind of jujube (*Zizyphus napeca*). The Egyptian lotus was a kind of water-lily, the centre of whose blossom was dried, crushed, and eaten, as also its round root. The seeds of another water-lily, whose blossoms were like a rose, were also eaten, as well as the lower stems of the byblus or papyrus, whose leaves were used for paper and other purposes. The mosquitoes were as great a nuisance in Egypt formerly as now. Herodotus says that some of the natives, to avoid them, slept on towers exposed to the wind; but in the marshes each man had a net, which served the double purpose of catching fish by day and acting as a mosquito-curtain at night.

For the early history of the country Herodotus had to depend upon his informants, who were usually the priests, especially those of Heliopolis — the Greek name by which he knew the oldest capital of Egypt, Êi-n̄-re, the On or Aon of the Hebrew Scriptures—the "City of the Sun." * The college of priests there was in fact the university of Egypt; and whatever faith we may place in their historical records, their proficiency in mathematics and astronomy was very considerable indeed. They asserted that the first

---

* The "Aven" of Ezek. xxx. 17; translated into the Hebrew Beth-shemesh—"House of the Sun"—Jer. xliii. 13. The silt of the Nile has now covered most of its monuments and buildings, but its massive walls may still be traced, and a solitary granite obelisk, said to be near 4000 years old, marks what was the entrance to the temple of the Sun.

kings of Egypt were gods, "who dwelt upon earth
with men." The last of this divine dynasty was
Horus, son of Osiris—whom the Greeks identified with
Apollo. The sufferings and death of Osiris were the
great mystery of the Egyptian creed. Herodotus had
seen his burial-place at Saïs, and knew the mysterious
rites with which, under cover of night, these sufferings
were commemorated. But he "will by no means
speak of them," or even mention the god by name.
Either the priests had enjoined secrecy upon him
as the price of their information; or perhaps, being
himself initiated in the Greek Mysteries, he had
a scrupulous reverence for those of Egypt. Osiris
was the great principle of Good, who slew his brother Typhon, the representative of Evil; and is pic-
tured in the hieroglyphic paintings as the great judge
of the dead. The first king of human race was Mên, or
Menes, the founder of Memphis, who began a line of
three hundred and thirty monarchs (including one
queen), whose names were read off to Herodotus from a
roll of papyrus. Eighteen were said to be Ethiopians.
Of most of these kings the priests professed to know
little more than the names; but Mœris, the last of
them, left his name to a large artificial lake, or reser-
voir, near the "City of Crocodiles," from which water
was conveyed to all parts of the neighbourhood. His
successor, Sesostris, is said to have conquered all Asia,
and even to have subdued Scythia and Thrace, in
Europe, marking the limits of his conquests by pillars
—two of which, in Palestine, Herodotus declares that
he himself saw.* Sesostris, after his return from his

---

* There is little doubt that these are the tablets still to be
seen near Beyrout.

conquests, met with somewhat too warm a welcome
from his brother, whom he had left viceroy of Egypt.
He invited the hero and his family to a banquet,
heaped wood all round the building, and set fire to it.
Sesostris only escaped by sacrificing (by the mother's
advice) two of his six sons, whose bodies he used to
bridge the circle of flame.   Having inflicted condign
punishment on his brother, he then proceeded to utilise
the vast multitudes of captives whom he had brought
with him.   By the employment of this forced labour
he changed the face of Egypt, completely intersecting
it with canals, and filling it with public buildings of un-
paralleled magnificence.   The second king after Sesostris bore a Greek name, but must be regarded as a very
apocryphal personage—Proteus, who was said to have
entertained at his court no less famous a visitor than
Helen, the heroine of the Trojan war.   For the Egyptian
priests had their version, too, of that wondrous Tale.
According to them, the Spartan princess was driven
by stress of weather to Egypt on her forced elopement
with Paris, while Troy was besieged by the Greeks,
in the belief that she was there.   King Proteus, when
he heard the story, gave Helen refuge, but dismissed
Paris at once with disgrace.   Herodotus accuses Homer
of knowing this legend, which was a more probable
version of the story than his own, and suppressing it
for poetical purposes, since he speaks of the long wan-
derings of Helen, and of Menelaus's visit to Egypt.
The priests told him that their predecessors had the
story from Menelaus himself, who went to Egypt to
fetch Helen, when he found, after the capture of Troy,
that she was not there.   Herodotus himself saw in the
sacred precincts at Memphis a temple to " Venus the

Foreigner," whom his Greek patriotism at once identified with Helen.

A story told at considerable length by Herodotus of
the next king, Rhampsinitus, is highly characteristic,
showing that sympathy of the Greek mind for clever
rascality which recalls Homer's manifest enjoyment of
the wily tricks of Ulysses in the 'Odyssey.' The story
of "The Treasury of Rhampsinitus," which has been
borrowed also by the Italian novelists, reads as if it
were taken from the 'Arabian Nights.'

King Rhampsinitus, having vast treasure of silver,
built for its safe keeping a chamber of hewn stone,
one of whose walls formed also the outer wall of his
palace. His architect, however, having designs on the
treasure, built a stone into the wall, which even one
man who knew the secret could easily displace. He
did not live long enough to carry out his views, but on
his deathbed explained the contrivance to his two sons,
for whose sake, he said, he had devised it, that they
might live as rich men, since the secret would make them
virtual chancellors of the royal exchequer through their
lives. After his death, the sons profited by his instructions to remove a considerable sum. The king, when
next he came to visit the room, missed his money, finding
it standing at a lower level in the vessels. This happened again and again, though the seals and fastenings
of the room were as secure as ever. At last he set a
man-trap inside. When the thieves next made their
usual visit, one of them found himself suddenly caught.
Seeing no hope of escape, he called to his brother to come
and cut off his head, to prevent his being recognised.
The brother obeyed; and, after replacing the stone,
made his way home with the head. When the king

entered at day-break, he greatly marvelled to see a head-
less trunk in the gin, while the building seemed still
to be fast closed all round.   To find out to whom the
body belonged, he ordered it to be hung outside the
palace-wall, and set a guard to watch, and bring before
him any persons they might observe lamenting over it.
The mother of the dead man, hearing of this desecra-
tion of a corpse that should have been a mummy, told
her surviving son that unless he contrived to rescue it,
she would go and tell the king that he was the robber.
Wearied with her continual reproaches, at last the
brother filled some skins with wine, loaded them on
asses, and drove them by the place where the guards
were watching the dead body.   Then he slily untied the
necks of some of the skins.   The wine of course began
to run out, upon which he fell to wailing and beating his
head, as if distracted, and not knowing to which donkey
he should run first to stanch the wine.   This highly
amused the guards, who ran eagerly to catch the wine
in all the vessels they could lay hands on.   Then the
driver pretended to get into a passion, and abused
them, upon which they did their best to quiet him.
At last, appearing to be put in good-humour again
by their raillery, he gave them one of the skins to
drink.   They invited him to help them with the
drinking, as they had helped him in putting the
skins in order.   As the wine went round, all got more
and more friendly, till they broached another skin, and
at last the guards all got so drunk that they went to
sleep on the spot.   In the dead of the night the thief
took down the body of his brother, laid it upon the
asses, and made off, having first remained long enough
to shave off the right whiskers of each of the men,—

which was considered a deadly insult. When the
king heard of this, he was more vexed than ever, and
determined to find out the thief at any cost. He bade
his daughter keep open house for all comers, and promise to marry the man who would tell her most to
her satisfaction the cleverest and wickedest thing he
had ever done. If any one told her the story of the
robbery, she was to lay hold of him. But the thief
was not to be thus outwitted. He procured a dead
man's arm, put it under his dress, and went to call on
the princess. When she put the question, he answered
at once that the wickedest thing he had ever done was
cutting off his brother's head in the king's treasury,
and the cleverest was making the guards drunk, and
carrying off his body. The princess made a grasp at
him, but in the darkness he left the arm of the corpse
in her hand and fled. But now the king was over-
whelmed with astonishment and admiration for the
man's cleverness, and made a proclamation of free
pardon and a rich reward, if the thief would declare
himself. He boldly came forward, and Rhampsinitus
gave him his daughter in marriage. "The Egyptians,"
he said, "are the wisest of men, and thou art the wisest
of the Egyptians."

Till the death of Rhampsinitus, Egypt enjoyed prosperity. Cheops, who succeeded him, and who built
the Great Pyramid, is said to have shut up all the temples, that his people might do nothing but work for
him; and he kept a hundred thousand labouring at
a time, who were relieved every three months. It
took ten years to make the causeway (of which traces
still remain) for the conveyance of stones, and another
twenty to build the Pyramid itself. The next kings,

Chephren and Mycerinus (Mencheres), likewise built pyramids, but on a smaller scale. The memory of Cheops and Chephren, in consequence of their oppressions, became so odious to the Egyptians, that they would not even mention their names; but upon Mycerinus, though he was just and merciful, there fell the punishment due for their sins. First he lost his only daughter, and then an oracle told him that he had but six years to live. He expostulated with the oracle, saying it was hard that he who was a good and righteous king should die early, while his father and uncle, who were so impious, lived long. The oracle answered—"For that very reason thou must die, for Egypt was destined to suffer ill for one hundred and fifty years, and thou hinderest the doom from being fulfilled." On this Mycerinus, finding it useless to be virtuous, determined to outwit the gods; so he lighted lamps at nightfall, and turned all the nights into days, and enjoyed them, as well as the days, in feasting in all pleasant places. Thus he lived twelve years in the space of six, making his six years one long day of continuous revel. The story of Mycerinus has been very happily treated in one of Matthew Arnold's earliest poems.*

> " I will unfold my sentence and my crime ;
> 　My crime, that rapt in reverential awe,
> I sate obedient, in the fiery prime
> 　Of youth, self-governed, at the feet of Law,
> Ennobling this dull pomp, the life of kings,
> 　With contemplation of diviner things.

---

* Its moral—if it has any—may be found in Moore's song,—

> " And the best of all ways
> 　To lengthen our days,
> Is to steal a few hours from the night, my dear."

" My father loved injustice, and lived long ;
  Crowned with grey hairs he died, and full of sway.
I loved the good he scorned, and hated wrong ;
  The gods declare my recompense to-day.
I looked for life more lasting, rule more high—
And when six years are measured, lo, I die !"

After him came a blind king named Anysis, during
whose reign Egypt was invaded by the Ethiopians, who
lorded it over the country for fifty years. He was succeeded by Sethos, a priest of Vulcan, who oppressed the
warrior caste, so that they refused to serve him when
Sennacherib, king of the Assyrians, invaded the country. But a vision in the sanctuary bid him be of good
cheer ; and when he went out to the frontier with an
army of citizens, trusting in divine aid, a number of
field-mice came in the night and gnawed the bow-
strings, quivers, and shield-straps of the enemy, so that
the Egyptians easily defeated them. Such is the dim
tradition which reached the historian of the mysterious destruction of the Assyrian host recorded in the
Scriptures. The mouse, according to some interpreters
of hieroglyphic language, was the symbol of destruction.
Thus far Herodotus had derived his information as to
early Egyptian history entirely from the priests. He computed that the reigns of these kings, as given him, would
require eleven thousand three hundred and forty years.

A revolution seemed to have occurred after the death
of Sethos, by which twelve provincial kings, like those
of the Saxon Heptarchy, reigned at once. Their great
work was a labyrinth near Lake Mœris, which struck
Herodotus as one of the wonders of the world—more
wonderful even than the Pyramids themselves. One
of the twelve, Psammetichus, at length managed to

depose the rest by the aid of Greek mercenaries. His
son, Nechos (Pharaoh Necho), is credited by Herodotus
with the first attempt to construct the canal to the Red
Sea, which was afterwards finished by Darius Hystaspes.
The canal, however, was more probably begun by Sesostris (Rameses II.), and there appears to be evidence
that it was choked by sand (which is still the difficulty with modern engineers), and reopened many times
— by the Ptolemies, for instance, and the Arabs.
Necho is mentioned in Scripture as having defeated
and slain King Josiah at Megiddo on his way to
attack the Assyrians.   Herodotus briefly notices the
victory, but calls the place Magdolus, after which he
says that Necho took the city of Cadytis, supposed
to be either Jerusalem or Gaza.   In a subsequent
expedition, which Herodotus does not mention, he
himself was defeated by Nebuchadnezzar, king of
Babylon, and lost all his conquests.   He was succeeded
by his son Psammis, and his grandson Apries (the
Pharaoh-Hophra of Jeremiah).   The latter had a long
and prosperous reign; but failing in an attack on the
Greek city of Cyrene, his army revolted from him, and
chose Amasis, an officer who had been sent to reason
with them, for their king.   Apries on this armed his
Greek mercenaries, amounting to thirty thousand men,
and went to meet the revolted Egyptians.   In the battle
which ensued he was defeated and taken prisoner by
Amasis, who finally gave him up to his former subjects,
with whom he was unpopular, and they strangled him.
Amasis was a coarse but humorous character, rather
proud than otherwise of his low origin.   Finding that
his subjects despised him for it, he broke up a golden
foot-bath, and made of it an image of one of the gods,

which the Egyptians proceeded to worship. He then
told them what it was made of, adding that " his own
fortune had been that of the foot-pan ;" thus anticipat-
ing the adage of Burns—

> " The rank is but the guinea-stamp,
> The man's the gowd for a' that."

When his courtiers reproved his undignified revels
in his hours of relaxation, whereas none could complain of his inattention to business, he met them with
the proverb, now common to most languages, that a
bow becomes useless if not sometimes unstrung. His
habits were certainly open to remark. To find money
for his pleasures before he came to the throne, he
occasionally took to highway robbery. The oracular
shrines were the police-offices of those times, and Amasis,
like other thieves, was cited in such cases before the
nearest oracle. Some of them would acquit, others
find him guilty. When he became king, he honoured
the oracles which had detected him very highly,
but the others he despised. But he was a great king,
in spite of his failings ; and Egypt is said to have
prospered more under him than under any of his
predecessors. One of his laws was, that every man
should appear once a-year before the governor of his
department, and prove, on pain of death, that he was
getting an honest livelihood. Herodotus says that Solon
borrowed this law from the Egyptians, and that it was
in force at Athens up to his own days. If this be
true, it fell into disuse soon after his time, as the
Athenians enjoyed a reputation above all nations in
the world for "gracefully going idle." We may at
least join in his remark, that this ordinance of Amasis

was "a most excellent custom," towards which our
modern civilisation is making timid approaches.   We
shall hear of this king again in connection with Polycrates, the despot of Samos.

The account which Herodotus here gives of the kings
of Egypt, however interesting and entertaining, must
be read with the full understanding that its value in
a historical point of view is about the same as that of
Livy's popular account of the early kings of Rome.
He was unacquainted with the Egyptian language, and
though the priests may not have purposely imposed
upon him, he had to depend on the anecdotes which
came to him through the medium of the caste of drago-
mans who were settled at Memphis.   In consequence
of this, the consecutiveness and general symmetry of
his account only serves to conceal some palpable mis-
statements.   Perhaps the greatest is that which makes
the builders of the Pyramids later in time than the
builders of the temples and other monuments.   Modern
investigations have tended to give great weight to the
authority of a native chronicler, spoken of with much
respect by early Christian writers, but who afterwards
fell into disrepute—Manetho, the high priest in the
days of Ptolemy Philadelphus.   His record is utterly
fatal to the main facts of the account given by Herodotus.   After dynasties of gods and heroes which
reigned more than sixteen thousand years, he brings
us to the builders of the Pyramids, whom Herodotus
places at a late period of his history, perhaps because
his Greek informants first became acquainted with the
monuments at Memphis itself.   He was probably furnished with two distinct lists of kings, both to a great
extent mythical, which he took to be separate and

successive dynasties. Cheops is almost certainly identical with Menes, the first human king of Herodotus, in whose time was effected the canalisation of the Delta. He is the traditional builder of the Great Pyramid, and Chemmis (the Sun) appears as one of his titles, at once connecting him with the sun-worship. The Pyramids are supposed to have been built before the time of Abraham, with the Pharaoh of whose times Achthoes of the 11th dynasty has been identified. The name Pharaoh itself continues the title assumed by Cheops, in its meaning of "children of the sun."

The Mycerinus of Herodotus is found to resolve himself into two kings, the Mencheres who built the Pyramids, and another much later king, of whom the story of turning night into day is told; a legend which may have originated in the torch-light festival of Osiris and Isis. Sesostris also resolves himself into two kings— Sethos, the great engineer and builder, and Rameses II., the great conqueror whose victories are recorded in the temples at Karnak and Luxor, and whose fallen statue at Luxor is the largest in the world. After him came Menephthes or Amenonoph, who has been identified with the Pharaoh of Exodus. The Shishak of Scripture has been confounded with Sesostris, but he came far too late, and is now identified with one Sesorchis. But the identification of any of these kings is as yet very uncertain.

Amongst other stories in the second book of Herodotus is one not quite presentable to the general reader, about a Greek beauty of doubtful repute, named Rhodôpis ("Rosy-cheek"), who had been brought as a slave to Egypt, and who was said to have built one of the Pyramids. Strabo embellishes her history by telling how, when this lady was bathing, an eagle carried off one of her sandals, and deposited it before the king of Egypt's throne, who was so struck by the suggested beauty of the foot which it fitted, that he sent for her and made her his queen. Such is the venerable antiquity of the story of Cinderella.

It is remarkable that Herodotus says nothing about the Great Sphinx, which strikes all modern travellers so forcibly, and which plays so prominent a part in the legends of the Greek Thebes. He must have seen it, but may have thought it (as he did other things in this mysterious country) "too sacred to mention." Its composite form is supposed to be emblematic of Nature, and connected in some way with the inundations of the Nile.

This second book of Herodotus brings the history of Egypt as an independent power to a close. It is an inexhaustibly rich mine of historical, archæological, and mythological wealth, on whose endless shafts and galleries modern discovery is ever throwing some new light. Formerly the deciphering of the hieroglyphic writing, in which all Egyptian sacred records were kept, was looked upon as all but hopeless, but since the key was supplied by the discovery of the famous Rosetta stone, which bore a Greek translation of its hieroglyphic inscription, scientific patience has been abundantly rewarded. Religion is essentially conservative, and older dialects and characters are continued in her service long after they have been superseded in secular use. We may cite as an example the Church Sclavonic dialect of the north, so valuable to philologists; the Sanscrit of India; the Latin still in use in the Roman Catholic ritual. Even in England we still use archaic characters for the inscriptions in our churches, but this is no doubt partly because of their greater picturesqueness.

CHAPTER IV.

CAMBYSES.

"The race of mortal Man is far too weak
To grow not dizzy on unwonted heights."
—GOETHE, "Iphigenia."

As soon after the death of Cyrus as the Persian arms
were at liberty, we find them directed against Egypt.
The former alliance of that country with Lydia might
seem an adequate cause for the invasion, but it is too
prosaic for the taste of Herodotus. He makes Cambyses, the son of Cyrus, march against Amasis because
he had practised on him a deceit something like that
of Laban towards Jacob, by sending him as a wife the
daughter of the late king, Apries, instead of his own.
Cambyses was, at all events, no safe subject for a prac-
tical joke, and Amasis might have found to his cost
that he had jested once too often.

Having purchased a safe-conduct through the desert
by swearing brotherhood with the chief of the Arabs,*
—by a process much the same as that described by
modern African travellers, which consisted in the con-
tracting parties mixing a little of their blood,†—Cam-

* "The safe-conduct granted by the chief of the Bedouins,"
says Kinglake, "is never, I believe, violated."
† "Several of our men made brotherhood with the Wezees, and

byses set out for Egypt. But death had put Amasis
beyond the reach of all enemies, and his son Psammenitus now reigned in his stead. Dire misfortunes had
been portended to the country by the unusual phenomenon of a shower of rain at Thebes. After an obstinate battle, Psammenitus was utterly routed. Herodotus went afterwards over the field, and saw there the
bones of the Persians lying in one heap, and those of
the Egyptians in another. He remarked that the skulls
of the former might be broken by a pebble, while those
of the latter resisted even a large stone. This observation he afterwards verified by personal inspection of
another battle-field, where a Persian force was subsequently defeated by the revolted Egyptians under
Inaros. He attributes the difference to the Egyptians
going bareheaded in the sun, while the Persians wore
turbans. The Persians followed up their victory by
the capture of the city of Memphis and of Psammenitus himself, on which occasion our author introduces
one of his characteristic pathetic stories. Cambyses
wishing, says Herodotus, "to try the spirit" of his royal
prisoner, ordered Psammenitus and some of the captive

the process between Bombay and the sultan's son, Keerenga,
may be mentioned. My consent having been given, a mat is
spread, and a confidential party or surgeon attends on each.
All four squat, as if to have a game at whist; before them are
two clean leaves, a little grease, and a spear-head; a cut is made
under the ribs of the left side of each party, a drop of blood put
on a leaf and exchanged by the surgeons, who rub it with butter
twice into the wound with the leaf, which is now torn in pieces
and strewn over the "brothers'" heads. A solemn address is
made by the older of the attendants, and they conclude the
ceremony by rubbing their own sides with butter, shaking
hands, and wishing each other success."—Grant's 'Walk through
Africa,' p. 108.

nobles to be brought out to the gates of the city. Then he caused the deposed king's daughter, and those of the nobles, to be led past, in the dress of slaves, carrying pitchers on their heads. The nobles wept at the sight, but Psammenitus only bowed his head. Next followed his son and two thousand other young Egyptians, going to execution with ropes round their necks. The people of Memphis had torn limb from limb the crew of a ship which Cambyses had sent with a summons to surrender, and this was his reprisal—ten for every man murdered. The nobles again wept and wailed loudly, but Psammenitus comported himself as before. But when he saw one of his former boon companions, an old man now reduced to beggary, asking alms from the soldiers, then his grief broke forth in tears, and he beat himself on the head. Cambyses was amazed that he should weep at the fate of his friend, and not at that of his daughter or son, and sent to ask him the reason of his strange conduct. Psammenitus answered, " O son of Cyrus, mine own misfortunes were too great for tears." Cambyses was sufficiently touched to order the life of the young prince to be spared, but the reprieve came too late. But from that time Psammenitus was treated better, and might, as Herodotus thinks, had he shown more tact, have been appointed governor of Egypt, since it was the Persian custom thus to honour fallen princes, even giving the kingdoms of rebel vassals to their sons.* But he was unwise enough to plot rebel-

---

* We have notable instances of this habit in Eastern monarchs recorded in Scripture. Jehoiakim is made king instead of his brother Jehoahaz, by Pharaoh-Nechoh (2 Kings xxiii. 34) ; Mattaniah instead of his nephew Jehoiachin, by Nebuchadnezzar (2 Kings xxiv. 17).

lion, and Cambyses, discovering this, put him to death.

And now the son of Cyrus entered on that career of impiety which was certain to have an evil end. He had the body of his enemy Amasis, who had escaped his vengeance while living, torn from its tomb, scourged, and committed to the flames—an act horrible to the Persians, who worshipped fire; horrible to the Egyptians, who looked upon that element as a devouring monster to whom it was impious to give their dead. Then, according to Greek poetical justice, he was seized by infatuation. He planned wild expeditions —one against "the Long-lived" Ethiopians, who dwelt far away to the south, and who might perhaps be identified with the modern Abyssinians (Heeren thinks, with the Somalis) by certain characteristics, such as tall stature, regular though black features, and a great love of animal food. Whoever they were, they are the subject of one of our author's most characteristic narratives. Cambyses sent envoys to them—men of the tribe of "Fish - eaters," who knew their language— with presents for their king; a purple robe, a collar and armlets of gold, and a cask of palm-wine, tokens of his goodwill, as "the things in which he himself most delighted." The Ethiopian king—who was elected for his stature and beauty — made answer almost in the words of Joseph to his brethren: "Surely to search out the land are ye come hither." He asked how the purple robe was made; and when they explained the mystery of the dye, he said that the Persians' garments, like themselves, were deceitful. When told the purpose of the golden collar and armlets, he chose to consider them as fetters, and remarked that

"the Ethiopians made them stronger." In fact, as
Herodotus declares, the envoys saw men afterwards in
prison actually wearing fetters of a metal which was
there so plentiful. Only the wine he highly approved
of, and asked what the king of Persia ate, and how
long men lived in that country. When he heard that
corn was the staple food, and that it grew out of the
earth, and that eighty years was considered a long life,
he replied that he did not wonder at the king's dying
so young if he "ate dirt," and that nothing, he was
persuaded, could keep him alive even so long, except
that excellent liquor. He sent back in return an
unstrung bow, with advice that, when the Persians
could find a man to bend it, they should then think
of attacking the "Long-livers."

Against this distant tribe, however, the Persian king
set out with a vast army, without bestowing a thought
on his commissariat. Before he had accomplished a
fifth of the distance the provisions failed, but he still
pushed on. The army fed on the sumpter-beasts till
they were exhausted; then on herbs and grass, till
they came to the sandy desert, where vegetation
ended. At last, when he heard of cannibalism in
the ranks, Cambyses thought it was time to return;
but he succeeded in bringing back only a small
remnant of his host. Another expedition, sent against
the temple of Ammon, in the great Oasis, fared even
worse, for no news came of it more. It perished, our
author thinks, in a sandstorm—more probably from
want of water. But Cambyses' heart was hardened.
When he returned from his ill-starred march, he found
the Egyptians holding high festival. This greatly
incensed him, for he thought they were rejoicing at

his defeat. But they were innocently celebrating the incarnation of their national god Apis or Epaphus, who was said to appear from time to time in the similitude "of a calf that eateth hay," and whose "avatar" in that form was denoted by certain sacred marks known to his priests. Cambyses was still more angry when he heard the real cause of this national jubilee : he had the priests scourged all round, forbade the people to rejoice on pain of death, and, to crown all, fell on the sacred beast and wounded him with his dagger, so that he pined away and died. From this precise date, as the Egyptians averred, the madness of Cambyses took a more decided character. But his acts, however unaccountable to a Greek mind, seem to have been little more than those of an Eastern despot of fierce passions and naturally cruel disposition. First he had his brother Smerdis put to death, and then he killed his sister because she mourned for Smerdis. He had sent this brother back to Persia because he excited his jealousy by being the only Persian who could just move the Ethiopian's bow ; and then, having dreamed that he saw Smerdis sitting on his throne and touching heaven with his head, he sent a nobleman named Prexaspes to Susa, who slew him according to his instructions. The story of the murder of the sister was differently told by the Persians and Egyptians. The former said that Cambyses, in the presence of his sister, had set a puppy to fight a lion-cub. The dog was getting the worst of it, when another of the same litter broke the cord that tied him, and came "to help his brother," and both of them together mastered the young lion. Cambyses was amused, but his sister wept, and said that she could not but think of Smerdis, who had no brother to help him. For this speech he killed her. The Egyptians said that the pair were seated at table, when the sister took a lettuce, and, stripping its leaves off, asked Cambyses whether it looked better with its leaves off or on? He answered, "With its leaves on." "Then why," said she, "didst thou strip of its leaves the stem of Cyrus?" A furious kick which followed this remark was the cause of her death. In fact, Cambyses had now become dangerous to all about him. Crœsus, whom he had brought with him to Egypt, had more than one narrow escape. On one occasion officers were sent to put him to death, but they, knowing their master's moods, only pretended to have done it, and produced Crœsus alive as soon as Cambyses was heard to regret the order. He was well pleased that his friend had not been killed, but the disobedience cost the guards their lives. Another time he shot the son of Prexaspes through the heart to prove the steadiness of his hand, merely because the father had told him, in answer to a question, that the Persians said he was rather too fond of wine. Probably for some similar offensive remark he buried up to their necks twelve of his nobles—a cruel process still practised in the East under the name of "tree-planting." * And he grew more and more profane. He opened tombs and unrolled mummies like a modern

* "Feti-Ali-Shah once sent for Astra-chan, one of his courtiers, and with an appearance of great friendship took him round his garden, showing him all its beauties. When he had finished the circuit, he appealed to Astra-chan to know 'what his garden still lacked?' 'Nothing,' said the courtier; 'it is quite perfect.' 'I think differently,' replied the king; 'I must decidedly plant a tree in it.' Astra-chan, who knew the king's meaning only too well, fell at his feet and begged his life, which he obtained only at the price of surrendering to the king the lady to whom he was betrothed."—Rawlinson, ii. 361, note

virtuoso. He made sport of the pigmy images of Pthah,
or Vulcan, whose ludicrous ugliness must have presented
the grim humorist with an irresistible temptation,* and
other sacred idols he burnt. Herodotus expresses himself much shocked at all this; but he might have
known that the Persians were in general iconoclasts.
It is possible that Cambyses was inspired with the
same destructive zeal which induced the more modern
Puritans to clear away the saints from the niches of
our cathedrals. But as a Greek, our author would
sympathise with the Egyptians. It is hard for us to
judge how far some of the cruelties reported of Cambyses may have been the invention of the outraged
priests. He has recorded, in another part of his work,
an anecdote which illustrates at once the character of
Cambyses and the general incorruptibility of the royal
judges of Persia. One of these, named Sisamnes, was
found to have accepted bribes. Cambyses, with the
facetious cruelty so common to tyrants of his type,
had him flayed, and his skin stretched over the seat
which he had occupied while administering the law.
He then appointed his son to the vacant post, charging
him at the same time never to forget "on what kind
of cushion he was sitting."

The modern reader will agree with Herodotus that
it is at least right to treat with delicacy the peculiar
usages of others. Aristotle quotes one of his anecdotes
to illustrate the opinion of those who held that all
right and wrong were conventional. King Darius
Hystaspes called certain Greeks into his presence,
and asked them what they would take to eat their
dead fathers? They said that they would do it for

* See the woodcuts and note, Rawlinson, ii. 434.

no consideration whatever. Then he asked a certain tribe of Indians what they would take *not* to eat the bodies of their fathers, but to burn them like the Greeks? They cried aloud, and begged him not to blaspheme. So Sir John Lubbock, in his 'Prehistoric Times,' relates that the Tahitians think it indecent to dine in company; and that as soon as a child is born he is accounted the head of his family, and takes precedence of his father. And the tyranny of public opinion in matters indifferent, of which we complain so often, finds its strongest exemplification among the semi-brutal savages of Australia.

The death of Smerdis had come to the knowledge of but few persons in Persia, and while Cambyses was absent in Egypt, the priest-caste of the Magi made a bold attempt at a revolution. It is probable that under Cyrus and Cambyses this caste, with their peculiar tenets, had been discouraged. A certain Magian, who was a kind of groom of the palace, had a brother who resembled greatly the dead Smerdis, and who (according to Herodotus) bore the same name.* Patizethes seated this brother on the throne, and sent out a proclamation that henceforth all men were to do homage to Smerdis the son of Cyrus, and no longer to Cambyses. When Cambyses heard of this, he thought that Prexaspes had not done his errand, and that it was really his brother Smerdis who had revolted against him; but Prexaspes satisfied him that his orders had been duly executed, and that this

---

* The Behistun inscription gives the name as Gomates, and does not speak of two brothers. Mr Rawlinson seems to prove clearly that the revolution was a religious one, though nothing to that effect appears in Herodotus.—See his Essay, iii. 548.

was a usurper personating the dead prince. He was
at once struck by remorse, seeing that his fratricide
had been useless, for his dream was so far fulfilled
that a man called Smerdis sat on his throne; and he
prepared to march at once in person to Susa to quell
the rebellion. As he was mounting his horse, the
knob of his sword-sheath fell off, and the bare point
of the weapon pierced his thigh, exactly as he had
pierced with his dagger the god Apis. His wound
brought him to his senses, and he solemnly conjured
the Persian nobles to prevent the empire from passing to the Medes, confessing that he had killed his
brother Smerdis, and that therefore the present occu-
pant of the throne must be an impostor. The wounded limb soon mortified, and Cambyses died in Egypt,
leaving no issue. Before his death, he asked the name
of the village where he lay. He was answered that
it was called "Ecbatana." Then he knew that he
should die; for an oracle had long ago predicted that
he should die at Ecbatana,—which he naturally took
to be his own town in Media. The coincidence with
the death of our own Henry IV. in the "Jerusalem
chamber" is very curious.

> "It hath been prophesied to me many years
> I should not die but in Jerusalem,
> Which vainly I supposed the Holy Land;—
> But bear me to that chamber; there I'll lie,—
> In that Jerusalem shall Harry die." *

* 'Henry IV.,' Part 2, Act iv. sc. 4.

CHAPTER V.

" In the theatre of the World
   The people are actors all.
   One doth the sovereign monarch play ;
   And him the rest obey."—CALDERON.

THE jealous hatred which Cambyses bore to his
brother Smerdis was so well known, that the Persians
did not believe his dying declaration that the person
who had seized his throne was an impostor. They
accepted him as the true Smerdis, son of Cyrus. Such
impostures are possible enough in a credulous age. A
false Demetrius plays an important part in the history
of Russia. There were many who disbelieved the fact
of the two English princes having been smothered in
the Tower ; and many more, at quite a recent date,
have believed that Louis XVII. escaped his jailers,
and grew up to manhood. The secluded life of an
Eastern monarch would give such an imposture additional chances of success.

The Magian usurper reigned for eight months under
the name of Smerdis, giving great satisfaction to most
of his subjects, for under him " the empire was peace."
He remitted the heaviest taxes, and enforced no mili-

tary conscription. At last his imposture came to light.
Otanes, a Persian nobleman, whose daughter was one
of his wives, was informed by her that her husband
had no ears. Now the Magian was known to have lost
his for some offence in the time of Cyrus.* The result
of this revelation was, that Otanes headed the famous
conspiracy of the seven nobles, of whom Darius, the
son of Hystaspes, sprung from a collateral branch of the
royal family, and probably the next legal heir, was
one. While they were concocting their plan of attack,
a tragical event happened which made immediate action
necessary. The Magians, knowing how cruelly Prexaspes had been treated by Cambyses,† thought it
their interest to conciliate him, and prevailed upon
him to mount on a tower of the palace-wall, and make
a speech to the people below, who had grown suspicious,
to the effect that their present king was the true Smerdis, the son of Cyrus. But in this they made as fatal a
mistake as Shakespeare's Brutus and Cassius did when
they allowed Mark Antony to speak at Cæsar's funeral.
Prexaspes, instead of lying to please the Magians, proclaimed aloud the real state of the case, and then threw
himself from the tower, and was killed on the spot.

---

* This is the mildest form of mutilation, as the feature seems
more ornamental than useful, except to those savage tribes in
whom the muscle that moves the ear is developed. It was practised in England as late as the seventeenth century, for such
offences as Nonconformity, Petty Treason, Libel, and the like.
Prynne is a well-known instance. It is common now in Africa,
and is said to give the head the look of a barber's block, but to
be attended with no great inconvenience. The False Smerdis,
as has been said, never went abroad, and probably wore his
turban low on his head.

† See p. 71.

The seven conspirators gained the presence of the false king and his brother with no great difficulty, but within they met with such resistance that two were badly wounded before they succeeded in despatching them. The others cut off the Magians' heads, carried them forth, and showed them to the populace. A general massacre of the Magian caste followed, which lasted till the night. Few of them survived this St Bartholomew of Susa. During the annual festival held henceforth under the name of Magophonia, which we might call the "Median Vespers," none of the hated class dared be seen abroad, though tolerated at other times.

The seven noblemen, according to Herodotus, now resolved themselves into a debating society, for the purpose of discussing different forms of government. That is to say, he here avails himself of an author's favourite licence to propound theories of his own. His sympathies are plainly with democracy, but historical exigencies obliged him to admit that monarchy was adopted. They agreed that one of the seven should be king, and the rest his peers, having free access to the royal presence on all but certain stated occasions. It was then arranged that all should ride their horses to an open place at sunrise, and choose as king the man whose horse was the first to neigh. This was really an appeal to the Sun, to whom the horse was sacred. The omen fell to Darius, by the cunning management of his equerry, and he was at once hailed as king. When he was established in the kingdom, he is said to have set up the figure of a man on horseback, with a commemorative inscription. The story may have been invented subsequently, to account for this work of art, as often happens.

Most valuable light has been thrown on the history
of Darius by the discovery of the great Behistun inscription. On the western frontier of the ancient
Media there is a precipitous rock 1700 feet high,
which forms a portion of the Zagros chain, separ-
ating the table-land of Iran from the valley of the
Tigris and Euphrates. The inscription can only be
reached with difficulty, as it is 300 feet from the
base of the rock. It is in three languages, — old
Persian, Babylonian, and Scythian,—executed, according to Sir H. Rawlinson, in the fifth year of Darius,
B.C. 516. The wedge-shaped letters of the Persian
copy were deciphered with infinite pains by this great
archæologist. Darius mentions in it, under the name
of Gaumata, a Magian who personated Bardes * (as he
calls him), the son of Cyrus, and says that he slew him
by the help of Ormuzd, the Good Spirit, and thus
recovered an empire that belonged to his own family,
restoring to the Persians the religion which they had
lost by the Magian intrusion. He also records that
after this he was engaged in quelling a general revolt
of the provinces. The main facts accord with those
of Herodotus, though there is some difference in the no-
menclature. The end of the inscription invokes a curse
on any one who might injure it, and this has probably
tended to preserve it; just as the curse on Shakespeare's
monument, at Stratford-on-Avon, may have conduced

---

* The *s*, whether at the beginning or end of Persian names,
is commonly only a Greek addition. So Bardy(a)—the vowel
being pronounced though not written—is *S*merdis, Gaumat(a)
becomes Gomates, Vashtasp(a) Hystaspes, &c.—See Rawlinson,
I. 27-29, note.

to prevent officious veneration from "moving his bones."

Darius was the first monarch of Persia who regulated the revenues, and assigned the sum that each satrapy ought to pay to the royal treasury. This caused the haughty Persian aristocracy to say of him, in their contempt for red tape, that Cyrus had been a father to the state, Cambyses a master, but Darius was "a huckster, who would make a gain of everything."

There can be no question that Herodotus had access, either personally or through friends, to the royal records of Persia, or copies of them. He gives a complete list of the various satrapies into which the empire was divided, of the several subject nations which it comprised, and the form and amount of their tribute. The Persians themselves, it must be remarked, like the Magyar grandees in Hungary formerly, were exempt from taxation, and only bound to military service. He says that the Indians, the most numerous race of all, paid into the royal treasury three hundred and sixty talents in gold dust, and that the whole annual revenue was computed at fourteen thousand five hundred and sixty talents, besides a fraction—more than three millions and a half of our money. But it must be considered that this corresponds to the modern Civil List, serving only to defray the expenses of the Court. These Indians must not be supposed to be those of the Peninsula, but rather those of Scinde and the Punjab. The gold which they brought into the royal treasury was said to come from a great desert to the eastward. In this desert there were ants—"bigger than foxes"—and in their hills the gold was found. To procure it the gold-hunters took camels, chiefly

females with young ones, with which they proceeded
to the place at the hottest time of day, when the
ants were in their holes, filled their bags with the aurif-
erous sand, and then hurried back to escape the pursuit of the ants; the female camels leading the way, as
anxious to get back to their young ones. The existence of these gigantic ants has been asserted by comparatively modern travellers, but it seems probable
that they must have been really ant-eaters, which
burrowed in the hills, and which some informants of
Herodotus may have seen.

Amongst the barbarian tribes in dependence on Persia, he mentions one called the Padæans, who, like the
Massagetæ before mentioned, allowed none of their sick
to die a natural death. The horrible story is quaintly
told. " If a man is taken ill, the men put him to death
to prevent his flesh being spoiled by his malady. He
protests loudly that he never felt better in his life ; but
they kill and eat him notwithstanding. So, if a woman
is ill, the women who are her friends do to her in like
manner. (The decent division of the sexes is worth remarking.) If any one reaches old age—a very uncommon occurrence, for he can only do so on condition
of never having been ill—they sacrifice him to the
gods, and afterwards eat him." Marco Polo, the
Venetian traveller, writing about 1500, found the
practice existing in Sumatra, where the relations as-
sembled in the sick man's house, suffocated him, and
then ate him, as he describes it, "in a convivial
manner." Among other wonders he mentions Arabian
sheep (the forefathers, no doubt, of our "Cape" breed)
which had tails three cubits long, for which the shep-
herds made little trucks to keep them off the ground

—"each sheep having a truck of his own." The
mention of remarkable countries and productions leads
Herodotus to observe that, while the Greeks have
the finest climate, as inhabiting the middle of the
earth, yet the farthest inhabited regions have the
finest productions — tin, amber, and gold coming,
for instance, from the ends of the earth ; but in
respect of horses he gives the palm to the Nisæan
breed of Media. Palgrave, in his Travels in Arabia,
speaks of the horses of Nedjid as the "cream of the
cream" of equine aristocracy.

Soon after the accession of Darius, one of his seven
fellow-conspirators, Intaphernes, got into trouble. He
insisted on seeing the king during his hours of privacy,
and being denied, cut off the noses and ears of two of
the palace officials, and hung them round their necks.
This displeased the king so much that he condemned
Intaphernes and all the males of his family to death.
But Darius was touched with pity by the lamentations
of the wife of Intaphernes, and allowed her to choose
which of her family she would save. She chose her
brother — explaining, when the king showed some
astonishment at her selection, that such a loss could
not possibly be replaced, her father and mother being
dead. Pleased with her wit, Darius gave her the life
of her eldest son into the bargain. Sophocles adopts
the same curious sentiment in his tragedy of Antigone.
The general justice of Darius would lead to the suspicion that the crime of Intaphernes was of the nature
of high treason, otherwise his family would hardly
have been involved in his punishment.

The story of Demiocedes, a famous surgeon of Crotona, who was brought to Persia as a slave, is intro-

duced by Herodotus to find a motive for the attention
of the king being called to Greece. He had abundant
reasons besides, as the history shows; but our author
will not desert the theory of his choice, that Woman
is the mainspring in all human affairs. Democedes
had got into favour at court by successful treatment
first of Darius himself, then of Atossa the favourite
sultana. For this latter service he obtained leave to
name his own reward,—it was, to be allowed to visit
his home; and, as Darius wished also to conquer
Greece, in order that Atossa's desire of having some
of "those Lacedæmonian handmaidens of whom she
had heard so much" might be gratified, Democedes
was sent to make the tour of Greece and its colonies
on the Italian coast with a party of spies. When he
reached his native Crotona, he chose to remain there,
and was assisted by his fellow-townsmen against the
Persians who tried to take him back with them. He
bade the latter tell Darius that he was about to be
married to the daughter of Milo the wrestler; wishing
the king to know that he was a man of some mark in
his own country, where—as in some cases amongst us
moderns—athletics ranked even higher than science.
These spies were said to have been the first Persians
who visited Greece.

But Darius had no time to think of Greece just
then, as his hands were full with a revolt in Baby-
lonia and other provinces, which appears to have
assumed larger proportions than those known to
Herodotus. Samos was the first state which was unfortunate enough to draw upon itself the might of
the Persian arms. The cause of this war was a cloak.
When Cambyses was in Egypt with his army, one

Syloson, brother of Polycrates of Samos, was also
there in exile. He appeared one day at Memphis in
a scarlet cloak, to which Darius, who was then a plain
officer of the royal guards, took a fancy, and asked the
wearer to name his price. Syloson, in a fit of generosity, begged him to accept it as a present; and it
had no sooner been accepted than he repented of his
good-nature. As matters turned out, the cloak of
Syloson became as famous as that of Sir Walter
Raleigh. Raleigh "spoilt a cloak and made a fortune," by spreading out his for Queen Elizabeth to
walk on; Syloson, by giving his away, led the way
to the ruin of his country. For when Darius came
to the throne, Syloson introduced himself at court as
the hero of the cloak, and Darius asked him what he
could do for him in return. He requested to be put
in possession of his late brother's dominion in Samos.
Mæandrius, the secretary of Polycrates, who was at
present in possession, was a man who had had greatness thrust upon him. When Polycrates was murdered,
the secretary found himself in possession of Samos; and
wishing to be " the justest of men," set up an altar to
the god of Freedom, stipulating only that he should be
appointed its high priest as a condition of his establish-
ing democracy. Finding, however, that the " Irre-
concilables " of the period intended to prosecute him
for embezzlement, he had repented of his republican
generosity, and made himself master of the citadel and
city. Darius now sent out an expedition which put
his friend Syloson in possession of the island, but not
without an insurrection, which led to a terrible massacre of the people.

Babylon, according to the Behistun inscription, re-

volted from Darius twice—once in the first and again
in the fourth year of his reign.   It is difficult to identify with either of these occasions the revolt now
mentioned by Herodotus.   According to his account,
—which in this instance must be regarded rather as
romance than history—so determined was the attempt,
that the Babylonians strangled most of their women, in
order to reduce their population, in preparation for the
expected siege.   Darius soon sat down before the city,
but the walls defied his utmost power; and the besieged
began to jeer the Persians, telling them that "they
would never take the city until mules foaled."
However, in the twentieth month of the siege, a
mule belonging to Zopyrus, a Persian of rank, did
foal—an event perhaps not physically impossible;
and Zopyrus thought that there must have been
something providential in the taunt of the Babylonians, and that now the city might be taken.   The
sequel, whether true or not in an historical sense, is
singularly illustrative of the chivalrous self-devotion
of the Persian nobility in the interests of their monarch.   Zopyrus proceeded to cut off his own nose and
ears, clipt his hair close, got himself scourged, and in
that state presented himself to Darius, and laid his
plan before him.*   Darius was greatly shocked at his
retainer's maltreatment of himself, but as it was too
late to mend the matter, made the proposed arrangement.   Zopyrus was to pretend to desert to the Babylonians, telling them that Darius had so ill-used him
because he had advised him to raise the siege.   The
Babylonians would probably believe him, and intrust

* The town of Gabii, according to Livy, was taken by the
Romans by a very similar stratagem.

him with the command of a division. Darius must then be willing to sacrifice a few thousands of his worst soldiers to give the Babylonians confidence in Zopyrus, who, when he had the game safe in his hands, would open the gates to the Persian army. All turned out according to the programme. Zopyrus admitted the Persians, who took the city. Darius did his best to destroy the formidable walls, and had three thousand of the leading rebels impaled; but not wishing to depopulate the city, procured from the neighbouring nations fifty thousand women to make up for those whom the Babylonians had sacrificed. As for Zopyrus, the king loaded him with honours and made him governor of Babylon; but he was wont to say,—more scrupulous than Henry IV. of France, who changed his religion to procure the surrender of the capital, thinking Paris " well worth a mass,"—that he would rather have Zopyrus unmutilated than be master of twenty Babylons.

CHAPTER VI.

"They dwell
In wattled sheds on rolling cars aloft,
Accoutred with far-striking archery."
— ÆSCHYLUS, "Prometheus."

HAVING disposed of Babylon, Darius next bethought himself of the Scythians. He had an old national grudge against this restless race, for having overrun Asia in the days of Cyaxares the Mede. The Behistun inscription only mentions the quelling of a revolt of the Sacæ, or Scythian subjects of Persia; but Herodotus speaks of an expedition on a vast scale against the independent nation.

The Scythians were, according to Herodotus, a people whose seat was in the steppes of northern Russia, more widely spread than the present Cossacks of the Don, but without any definite boundaries, sometimes encroaching on their neighbours and sometimes encroached upon by them, like the Tartar hordes at this day. Their name has been supposed by some to be a synonym for "archers." Their habits were very like those of the terrible Huns and Magyars who overran part of Europe in the last agonies of

Rome and afterwards; but the difficulty of identify-
ing a modern and civilised race with an ancient and
barbarous one, is shown by the dissimilarity of the
handsome and chivalrous Hungarians with their hideous and unkempt progenitors. They seem to have
inherited from them little besides their love of horse-
flesh—in the civilised sense.

That the Scythians disappeared from history, when
history itself was at its lowest ebb, is no proof that
they exist nowhere now. Their language, specimens
of which are given by Herodotus, undoubtedly be-
longs to that of the Indo-Germanic family. Their
connection with the Sacæ is established. Some con-
nect the Sacæ with the Saxons, others also with the
Sikhs of northern India. It would indeed be strange
if it were discovered from critical philology and ar-
chæology that the English were pitted against their
cousins at Sobraon, Chilianwallah, and Gujerat, and
recovered India through their aid afterwards; and that
some of our Saxon ancestors were those who fought
best on the losing side at Marathon and Platæa. Certain it is that nearly all the now dominant races of
mankind seem to have swarmed, at longer or shorter
intervals, from some mysterious hive about or beyond
the Caucasus. History records some of the waves of
their western or eastern progress. Before the Scythians came a swarm of Cimmerians, sweeping over Asia
Minor in the time of the predecessors of Crœsus. Their
name is still retained in the Crimea and Krim Tartary.
They reappear as Cimbri in the latter days of the Roman republic, to which they were very near giving the
finishing stroke. Then they are heard of in Schleswick
and Jutland, and in Wales it is just possible that at

the present day they call themselves Cymry. Before
their coming a horde of Celts or Gauls had fallen on
Rome, and another invaded Greece later on, leaving
permanent settlements in Lombardy and Asia Minor.

In earlier history these tidal waves of population
came at long intervals, so that the damage they did
was reparable, and the silt they left behind them only
strengthened the ground; but in the latter days of the
Roman Cæsars, they succeeded one another so quickly
that the Empire was swamped, and when the disturbance had subsided, the earth wore a face that was
strange and new. The repentant sons of those savage
children of the night, calling themselves English,
French, Germans, and so forth, are now endeavouring
to atone for their fathers' delinquencies by painfully
diving after the relics of lost civilisations, and preserving whatever they can find with religious veneration
for the use and delight of ages to come. By degrees
we are opening up Greece, Italy, Assyria, Persia, India,
Egypt, and discovering to our dismay that much of our
boasted civilisation is but a parody on what prevailed
centuries or millenniums ago; and that, with all our
culture, we have still much barbarism to unlearn.

The Scythians described by Herodotus, like the
Parthians who defeated the Roman legions, are a race
of archers on horseback. From them the Greeks may
have derived their fables of the Centaurs. As a pas-
toral people, they were generally averse to the tillage
of land, and moved about with their herds from one
feeding-ground to another, carrying their skin-covered
huts on carts. That the Sarmatians were allied with
them appears from the fable which traces their descent
to the union of Scythians with Amazons, those wonder-

ful viragos whose manlike habits are still kept up by the women of some Tartar tribes.

To account for the origin of the Scythians, Herodotus gives two fables. According to one, a certain Targitäus, a son of Jupiter, and grandson by his mother's side of the river Borysthenes or Dnieper, was the first man in Scythia. He had three sons. At first they were all equal, when there fell from heaven four implements of gold—a plough, a yoke, a battle-axe, and a goblet. The eldest approached to take them, when they broke out into flames, and he durst not touch them. The second was rejected in like manner. The youngest fared better: he was able to handle the gold and to carry it off. This was a sign that he should be the king.* From the three

---

* A somewhat similar story was told to Speke by Rumanika, king of Karaguè.

"Before their old father Dagara died, he had unwittingly said to the mother of Rogero, although he was the youngest born, 'what a fine king he would make;' and the mother in consequence tutored him to expect to succeed, although primogeniture is the law of the land, subject to the proviso, which was also the rule with the ancient Persians, that the heir must have been born after his father's accession, which condition was here fulfilled in the case of all three brothers. . . . Rumanika maintained that Rogero was entirely in the wrong, not only because the law was against him, but the judgment of heaven also. On the death of the father, the three sons, who only could pretend to the crown, had a small mystic drum placed before them by the officers of state. It was only feather-weight in reality, but being loaded with charms, became too heavy for those not entitled to the crown to move. Neither of the other brothers could move it an inch, while Rumanika easily lifted it with his little finger. . . . He (Rumanika) moreover said that a new test had been invented in his case besides the ordeal of lifting the drum. The supposed rightful heir had to plant

brothers sprang the three Scythian tribes—the "Royal" Scythians from the youngest. According to the other legend, which emanated from a Greek source, Hercules, when he was carrying off the cattle of Geryon (who lived on an island near Cadiz in Spain), came to Scythia, and being overcome by frost and fatigue, wrapt himself in his lion's skin, and fell asleep. When he awoke his team of mares had disappeared. He wandered in quest of them till he came to a country called the Bush. Here he found in a cave a strange being, half woman, half serpent, who detained him with her by holding out hopes of his recovering his mares, which she had caught and hidden.*   Three sons were the

himself on a certain spot, when the land on which he stood would rise up like a telescope drawn out till it reached the skies. If he was entitled to the throne, it would then let him down again without harm ; but if otherwise, collapse and dash him to pieces. Of course as he survived the trial, it was successful. On another occasion a piece of iron was found in the ground, about the shape and size of a carrot. This iron could not be extracted by any one but Rumanika himself, who pulled it up with the greatest ease."—'Lake Victoria;' a compilation from the Memoirs of Captains Speke and Grant.

* These legends of serpent-women are not uncommon in German mythology. The following adventure is related by the brothers Grimm : "One Leonhard, who was a stammerer, but a good fellow, and of irreproachable morals, lost his way one day as he was visiting some underground vaults of the nature of catacombs. All at once he found himself in a delicious meadow, in the midst of which was playing a young girl, half concealed by the herbage. She invited him to come and rest by her side. Leonhard, out of pure politeness, obeyed her eagerly, and then became aware of a fact which the long grass had at first prevented his observing,—that the damsel, the upper part of whose body was white and beautiful, terminated below in a scaly and serpent-like tail. He wished to fly, but his legs

result of this strange intimacy—one called Agathyrsus, the other Gelonus, the other Scythes. Hercules, on his departure, left with the mother a bow, and a belt with a goblet attached to it. The son who could bend the bow was to inherit the land, the others to emigrate. Scythes, the youngest, bent the bow, and remained to be the father of the kings of Scythia, which accounted for the Scythian custom of wearing a goblet attached to the girdle.

In describing the geography of Scythia, of which

were immediately caught and embraced by her tail. Thus forced to listen, he now heard the poor creature's history. She was born a princess, and was enjoying court society, when a malicious enchanter charmed her into her present state, from which she could only be released on one condition, and that was, that she could prevail on some fair young man, who must be perfectly innocent, to give her three kisses. The youth must not be older than twenty-two. There was time for Leonhard to have fulfilled the conditions, for he would be twenty-three on that very day—in two hours more. But, unfortunately, he stammered, and the two hours were almost gone before he had made the necessary preliminary statement as to his birth. Then he gave her the first kiss. Upon that she was seized with violent convulsions, and rolled so wildly on the grass that he fled in alarm. He was, however, recalled by her supplications and promises, and gave her the second kiss. The effect of this was still more electric than that of the first. Her eyes burned like fire, she sprang up, her face glowed and her cheeks seemed bursting; she whirled about like a demoniac, and hissed, shrieked, and yelled like a very Melusina. Frightened out of his wits, the youth rushed away through the meadow and catacombs till the hideous object was out of sight; but after a time, reflecting that he might have made his fortune and married a princess, he turned to go back once more. It was too late; for, to his unspeakable chagrin, he just then heard a village clock strike twelve, which made him twenty-three years of age.—X. R. Saintine, 'La Mythologie du Rhin' (free translation).

Herodotus probably knew no more than he may have heard at the Greek factory at Olbia (near the site of the modern Kinburn), he is carried away by the interest of his subject, and launches out into a geographical digression, chiefly entertaining as a record of ancient notions, and as showing how facts become altered in passing from mouth to mouth. The " Scythia " of Herodotus seems to embrace " the basins of the Don, Dnieper, Dniester, and Boug, and the northern half of that of the Lower Danube "*—i.e., a great portion of Russia, Bessarabia, Wallachia, and Moldavia. He tells strange stories of the tribes who dwelt around Scythia, as far as the uttermost parts of Europe. The Issedonians and the Androphagi were given to cannibalism ; the former, like the Callatian Indians, feasting on their fathers, and keeping their skulls set in gold as heirlooms. This custom was, however, balanced with another, which would place them, as some might think now, in the van of progress —they gave women equal rights with men. The Neuri were said to change into wolves periodically; a tradition which still survives in the " wehr-wolf " of the Germans, and the " loup-garou " of the French. Livingstone relates that there were men in the country above the Zambesi who were supposed to become lions for a term, and that the souls of great captains were thought to pass into the king of beasts. But perhaps the story rose out of the fact that the Neuri wore wolf-skins in winter. There were people in the extreme north who slept six months in the year (Herodotus's informant may have said that there was night for six months), and who had goat's feet—that is, they may

* Heeren.

have worn moccasins. These may have suggested the
Satyrs of the Greeks. A common superstition also
placed a wonderfully good and happy people behind
the region of the north wind, called Hyperboreans.
So the "blameless" Ethiopians were supposed to
inhabit the extreme South. The Greeks believed in
goodness when a very long way from home.

Our author mentions slightly, and with some disdain, the legend (known also to other writers) of one of
these Hyperboreans, Abaris, who was said to have been
even a greater traveller than himself—who "walked
round the world with an arrow, without once eating."
But whatever may be thought of the latter part of
the story, it seems highly probable that in Abaris's
"arrow" we have a dim tradition of the magnetic
needle. Its properties were certainly known to the
Chinese long before Herodotus's date, and some
rumour of the marvel might have reached Europe.
The story tempts Herodotus into speculative cosmo-
graphy. He is dissatisfied with the map of Hecatæus,
who divided the habitable world into two equal portions, Europe and Asia, making it like a medal, with
the great river of Ocean for a rim; not that he himself
at all suspected the world of being a sphere, like some
of the later ancients, but that he thought the distribution of the continents manifestly unsound.

If Herodotus had been in the habit of rejecting
every tale that he did not believe, like some later
writers, we should have lost the valuable passage
which seems to prove that Africa was circumnavigated
twenty-one centuries before the time of Diaz and Vasco
de Gama. Pharaoh Necho, after giving up the Suez
canal as hopeless, sent a fleet of Phœnician ships down

the Red Sea, ordering them to return to Egypt by the
pillars of Hercules—that is, by the Strait of Gibraltar.
As these were their orders, it is to be presumed that
the route was already known.   They spent three years
in accomplishing their task, as they had to sow grain
on the way, and wait for the harvest.   Herodotus pro-
nounces their voyage apocryphal, because they reported
they had the sunrise on their right hand as they sailed
round Libya, but which proves indeed that they had
doubled the Cape of Good Hope.   Sataspes, a Persian,
tried to sail round Africa in the other direction, but
failed.   He had got beyond Cape Soloeis (Spartel) to
a country inhabited by a dwarfish people, who dressed
in palm-leaves ; and there, as he declared, the ship
stopped, and would go no further.   He had evidently
fallen in with the southerly trade-wind, and was not
aware that, in order to proceed, he ought to have
pushed across towards the South American continent.
He met with a fate worse even than that of some later
discoverers : he was not only disbelieved, but put to
death on his return.   Darius appears to have taken a
great interest in such discoveries, and it was he who
sent Scylax the Carian down the Indus to explore the
Indian Ocean.*

Amongst the strange customs which Herodotus records of the Scythians was their manner of keeping
the anniversary of the burial of their kings.   They
slew fifty young men and fifty choice horses, stuffed

* This Scylax, or more probably a later writer who traded on
his name, brought home some remarkable travellers' stories.
He described an Indian tribe whose feet were so large that they
used them as parasols, and another whose ears were so capacious
that they slept in them.—See Rawlinson, I. p. 50, note.

the bodies of both, and set them up round the tomb in a circle, the men mounted on the horses, a ghastly body-guard for the royal ghost. Their great deity was the god of war, whom they worshipped under the shape of a scimitar. The Russian or Turkish vapour-bath would appear to have been another of their institutions; but Herodotus seems to confuse it with the process of intoxiçation by hemp - seed, which was known in early times. They were also distinguished by drunkenness and dislike of foreigners, like some of their supposed descendants, who are not yet cured of these weaknesses.

Against this nation Darius is said by Herodotus to have moved a vast army, bridging over the Thracian Bosphorus and the Danube with boats, and taking with him the Ionian fleet, to the custody of whose commanders he committed the bridge over the river, while he passed on into the northern wildernesses. The Scythians retreated before him towards the Tanais or Don. Then they led him such a long chase that at last his patience was worn out, and he sent to their king to demand that, as a man of honour, he should either stand and fight, or deliver earth and water in token of submission. The Scythian replied that he would soon send him some presents more to the purpose. These arrived in due course of time—a bird, a mouse, a frog, and five arrows. Darius at first thought that this signified a tender of homage; but Gobryas, one of the Seven, who had an older head, read the hieroglyphic letter as follows: "Unless you can fly like a bird, or burrow like a mouse, or swim like a frog, you will not escape the Scythian arrows." Darius took the hint and retreated.

But Scythian horsemen had reached his bridge before him, and tried to prevail on the Ionians to destroy it. Miltiades the Athenian, now tyrant of the Chersonese (of whom we shall hear again), called upon his fellow-Greeks to strike, once for all, a blow for freedom; to cut the bridge, and leave their Persian masters to perish. But he was overruled in the interest of Darius by Histiæus of Miletus, and the Persian army returned without irretrievable loss from its military promenade in pursuit of the impalpable Scythians. Megabazus remained behind to reduce the Thracian tribes in the neighbourhood of the Hellespont.

This leads our author to discuss the ethnology of Thrace. It appeared to him that if its numerous tribes had been only united, they would have been a match for any existing nation. His Thrace must nearly have comprehended the present limits of Roumelia, Bulgaria, Servia, Moldavia, and Wallachia. The Getæ or Goths, who were subdued by Darius on his way to Scythia, believed that when they died they went to a good spirit named Zalmoxis, to whom they sent a messenger every five years; that is, they sacrificed a man by tossing him in the air and catching him on points of lances. Another tribe, when a child was born, sat round him, bewailing the miseries he would have to undergo; while in a case of death they made a jubilee of the funeral, believing the departed to have attained everlasting happiness. The same belief was connected with a custom in another tribe corresponding to the "Suttee" of the Hindoos. When a man died there was a sharp contention amongst his widows which was the worthiest to be slain over his grave, and the surviving wives considered themselves as in disgrace.

They marked high birth by tattooing, like the South
Sea Islanders ; and thought idleness, war, and plunder
honourable, but agriculture mean. The nation in general worshipped only the gods of battle, of wine, and
of the chase. But the kings paid especial honour to a
god corresponding to Hermes or Mercury, or the German
Woden. Less was known of the tribes north of the
Danube. The Sigynnæ wore a dress like that of the
Medes, and possessed a breed of active, hardy, shaggy
ponies, the description of which answers to those of the
Shetland Islands. Or possibly some vague rumour of
the harnessed dogs of Kamskatka may have reached
the ears of our author. He does not think that the
Thracians could have been correct in saying that a
tract of country beyond the Danube was so infested
with bees as to be uninhabitable, as bees cannot bear
much cold. They may have meant mosquitoes.

Megabazus was now commissioned to transport
bodily to Persia the whole tribe of the Pæonians, who
lived to the north of Macedonia, of whose industry
Darius had conceived an exaggerated notion, by seeing
one of their women at Sardis bearing a pitcher on her
head, leading a horse, and spinning flax all at the same
time. He effected this task with no great difficulty;
but other tribes resisted his arms with success, and especially those who inhabited the Lake Prasias. These
must have been a relic of the most ancient population
of Europe. Their habits were precisely the same as
those of the singular people whose whole manner of
life has been brought to light by the discovery of
ancient piles in the lakes of Zurich in Switzerland,
and who appear to have inhabited nearly all the
comparatively shallow lakes that have hitherto been

examined. This pile - city of Prasias is thus described :—

"Platforms supported on tall piles were fixed in the
midst of the lake, approached from the land by a
single narrow bridge. Originally all the citizens in common drove the piles for the platform, but afterwards
every man drove three piles for every wife he married,
and they had each several wives. Each man had his
own hut on the platform, and his trap-door opening
through the scaffolding on the lake below. They tied
the little children by the leg to prevent their rolling
into the water." (The proportionate number of children's bones found in the Swiss lakes would argue that
this custom was but negligently observed in those
regions.) "They fed their horses and other cattle
upon fish, of which there was such an abundance that
they had only to let down a basket through the trap-
door into the water, and draw it up full."

What was the ultimate fate of this amphibious
colony we do not learn; but very many of the corresponding settlements in central Europe bear traces
of having been destroyed by fire. For the present
these lake-people were impregnable, and Megabazus
turned his attention to Macedonia, sending first to the
court of King Amyntas an embassy of seven noble
Persians to demand earth and water. Amyntas entertained them at a feast; but when their attentions to the
ladies of the court began to be offensive, his son Alexander, indignant at the insult, dressed up some Macedonian youths to personate the ladies, whom he had
managed to withdraw under promise of their return,
and assassinated the Persian envoys when heavy with
wine. An expedition was afterwards sent to inquire

after their fate, but Alexander conciliated the commander with hush-money and the hand of his sister in marriage. The royal family of Macedonia were of Argive origin, according to Herodotus; otherwise, he says, they would not have been allowed to contend at the Olympic games. This Greek descent was used subsequently by Philip of Macedon as a plea for his intervention in the affairs of Greece.

A casual notice of the founding of Cyrene leads Herodotus into Libya, whither we have no space to follow him. He touches on the known North African tribes, and glances at the unknown, relating many marvellous stories; in fact, his love for anthropology and geography makes him seize any excuse for imparting information. He wellnigh exhausts the world as known to the ancients, and might have wept, as Alexander did that he had no more worlds to conquer, that he had no more to describe. Of one remote and apocryphal region he confesses he knew nothing. He was not sure that the islands called the Cassiterides ("Tin-Islands") had any real existence; but he had been told that tin came "from the ends of the earth." Such is the sole notice which the great traveller has left of us or our ancestors; for it is probable that the Cassiterides were the coast of Cornwall.

CHAPTER VII.

" If gods will not misfortune send,
  List to the counsel of a friend ;
    Call on thyself calamity ;
  And that, from all thy treasures bright,
  In which thy heart takes most delight,
    Commit forthwith to deepest sea."
        —SCHILLER, "Ring of Polycrates."

THE original constitution of most of the Greek States
was a limited monarchy, though the king was emphati-
cally "hedged by divinity," since the founder of his
family was generally supposed to be a god. In time,
as the royal prestige wore out, this constitution was
generally superseded by an oligarchy, which lasted
until some ambitious individual, by courting the un-
privileged classes, managed to raise himself to the
supremacy.

In the fifth century before Christ there were so
many of these usurpers at the same time in Greece,
that it has been called the Age of Tyrants. Mr Grote
prefers to call them "despots ;" but the name matters
little if no sinister meaning is necessarily attached to
the word Tyrant. Their number at one time was a
fact in support of those who believe in social and

political epidemics. One of the most famous of them
was Polycrates of Samos. He was great in arms and
arts, and the poet Anacreon was the companion of his
revels, just as Goethe enjoyed his Rhenish with Charles
Augustus, the jolly Grand-Duke of Weimar. His prosperity was so perfect, that his friend King Amasis of
Egypt, as a prudent man, thought it his duty to give
him a solemn warning, and advised him to avert the
anger of the gods by sacrificing some object which
he held very precious. Polycrates chose out of his
abundant treasures a favourite emerald ring, which he
at once threw into the sea. Five or six days afterwards, a poor fisherman caught so magnificent a fish
that it struck him that it was only fit to set before a
king. To Polycrates, therefore, he presented it, with
many compliments. The tyrant, with his usual geni-
ality, made it a condition that the fisherman would
come and help him to eat it. He bashfully accepted
the honour. When the fish was served, behold ! the
emerald ring was there in its inside. The servants
were exceedingly glad that the king's lost ring was
found—possibly they had been charging each other
with stealing it ; but Polycrates looked serious, for
he felt that the gods had rejected his offering. He
thought it right to inform his friend Amasis of the
result. Amasis, with less generosity than foresight,
at once sent a herald to Samos to renounce the alliance of Polycrates, as he felt sure that the gods had
decreed his ruin, and did not wish to be himself
involved in it. The tale of the fisherman and the
ring has been transferred to Arabian fable.

Fortune still continued to smile on Polycrates, and
he overcame all his enemies by force or fraud. Some

Samians, whom he had driven out, managed to set on foot against him an expedition from Lacedæmon. The visit of these people to Sparta is characteristically told. They made a long speech there in the assembly, which they would have hardly done if they had known the Spartan temper better. The authorities made reply that they had forgotten the first half of their discourse, and could not understand the second. The Samians then held up an empty bag, merely remarking, "The bag wants flour." The Spartans said that the word "bag" was quite unnecessary—the gesture was enough. However, they sent a force to Samos to support the exiles; and Polycrates is said to have bribed them to return with leaden money gilt over. The existence of the story is singularly illustrative of the avarice as well as the gullibility of this people.

But the doom of Polycrates could only be deferred. Towards the end of the reign of Cambyses, he was unfortunate enough to excite the cupidity of Orœtes, the Persian satrap of Sardis, who proceeded to set a trap for him. Orœtes said that he feared the covetousness of Cambyses, and offered to deposit all his treasure with Polycrates. The latter sent his secretary to inspect it, who was shown some large chests full of stones, just covered with gold. Satisfied with this report, in spite of all the warnings of his daughter, Polycrates started for the court of Orœtes to fetch the treasure. The satrap at once arrested him, put him to a cruel death, and then impaled his dead body. But the murderer afterwards came to a violent end himself in the reign of Darius.

Another specimen of a tyrant, and this, too, in our common acceptation of the word, was Periander of

Corinth, the son of Cypselus. By his origin he was partly patrician and partly plebeian. At one time the government of Corinth was in the hands of a single family called the Bacchiadæ, who only intermarried with one another. But one of them happened to have a daughter called, from her lameness, Labda (from the Greek letter Λ (L), which originally had one leg shorter than the other), whom her parents were, on this account, obliged to marry out of the family to one Aëtion, a man of the people. In consequence of oracles which boded ill to Corinth from a son of Aëtion, the rulers sent ten of their number to despatch the infant as soon as he was born. When they came and asked to see the child, Labda showed it them, thinking their visit was only complimentary. They had agreed that whoever took the child first in his arms should dash it on the ground. Providentially, however, the babe smiled in the man's face who had taken him, so that he had no heart to kill it, but passed it on to his neighbour, and he to another, and so it went through all the ten. When the mother had carried the child indoors again, she overheard the party outside loudly reproaching one another with their faint-heartedness in not making away with it. Fearing from this that they would return, she hid the child away in a chest or corn-bin, so that when they re-entered they could not find him. From this escape be was called Cypselus or 'Bin.' When he grew up he made himself despot of Corinth, and ruled harshly, visiting the citizens with confiscations, banishment, and death. He reigned thirty years, and then his son Periander succeeded him, who, at first, was a mild ruler, until he sent to Thrasybulus, despot of Miletus, to ask him the best way of governing his people. Thrasybulus took the Corinthian herald forth into the fields, and as he passed through the corn, still questioning him about Corinthian affairs, he snapped off and threw away all the ears that overtopped the rest. He walked through the whole field doing this, till the damage was considerable. After this he dismissed his visitor without a word of advice. When the messenger returned to Periander, he said that he had been sent on a fool's errand to a madman, who gave him no answer, but only walked through a field spoiling his wheat by plucking off all the longest ears.* Periander said nothing; but he understood the meaning of Thrasybulus, which was, that he was to govern by cutting off all the foremost citizens. After this he became a much worse tyrant than his father, and finished the work which he had begun. On one occasion he stripped all the women of Corinth of their clothes. Having sent to consult an oracle of the dead† about some lost property, the shade of his wife Melissa (whom he had put to death) appeared to him, and said that she was cold, and had literally nothing to put on; for the robes buried with her were of no use, since they had not been burnt. So he made proclamation that all the matrons should go to the temple of Juno in full dress, and there having surrounded them

* The English reader will remember the words of the gardener in Shakespeare :—

> " Go thou, and like an executioner,
> Cut off the heads of too fast-growing sprays,
> That look too lofty in our commonwealth."
>   —' Richard II.,' Act. iii. sc. 4.

† Hence the word "necromancy." The parallel of Saul, the witch of Endor, and the ghost of Samuel, is at once suggested.

with his guards, took all their clothes from them, and
burnt them as an offering to his dead queen.

The relations of Periander with his younger son
Lycophron form one of the most touching episodes in
Herodotus. The lad had learnt the fact of his mother's
murder, and from that time would neither speak to his
father nor answer him. The father at last banished him
from his house. He even sent warning to the friends
with whom his son took refuge, that all who harboured
him did so at their peril—nay, that any who even spoke
to him should pay a fine to Apollo. The lad wandered
miserably from one to the other, and at last was found
lying in the public porticoes. Then Periander himself
went to him, and upbraided him with his folly in de-
priving himself by his obstinacy of a princely home.
Lycophron only answered by reminding his father that
he had now himself incurred the forfeit to the god. Periander saw that the case was hopeless, and sent him to
Corcyra for safe keeping. But when he found himself
growing old, and unequal to the cares of government,
and saw that his elder son was quite incompetent,
he sent to offer to resign in Lycophron's favour. No
reply came. Then the father sent his favourite sister
to treat with him, and try to soften his heart. Lycophron's answer was that he would never set foot again
in Samos while his father lived. Periander humbled
himself so far as to offer to retire himself to Corcyra,
and allow the son to take his place. To this Lycophron
agreed; on hearing which the people of Corcyra murdered him, in dread of receiving as their master the
terrible Periander.

A pleasanter story in connection with him will be
best told, as nearly as may be, in the old historian's

own words, with a little retrenchment of his diffuseness.

ARION AND THE DOLPHIN.

In Periander's days there lived a minstrel of Lesbos, Arion by name, who was second to none as a player on the lute. This Arion, who spent most of his time with Periander, sailed to Italy and Sicily, and having earned by his minstrelsy great store of treasure, hired a Corinthian ship to go back to Corinth—for whom should he trust rather than the Corinthians, whom he knew so well. When the crew were out at sea, they took counsel together to throw Arion overboard, and keep his treasure. But he divined their intent, and besought them to take his money, but spare his life. But the shipmen refused, and bade him either straightway kill himself on board, so that he might be buried on shore, or leap into the sea of his own freewill. Then Arion, being in a sore strait, begged, since it must be so, that he might don his vestments, and sing one strain standing on the quarterdeck; and when he had ended his song he promised to despatch himself. [He asked to put on his sacred garb, knowing that thereby he should gain the protection of Apollo.] The seamen consented, as well pleased once more to hear the master of all singers, and made space to hear him, withdrawing into the midship; and he chanted a lively air, and then plunged overboard, all as he was. So they sailed away to Corinth, and thought no more of Arion. But, lo! a dolphin took the minstrel up on his back, and landed him safely at the promontory of Tænarus in Laconia, whence he made his way to Corinth, all in his sacred robes, and told there all that had befallen him. But

Periander did not believe him, and kept him under
guard. At last the shipmen came, and when Periander
asked them what had become of Arion, they said they
had left him safe and sound at Tarentum, in Italy.
Then Periander produced Arion in his vestments, just
as he was when he leapt overboard, and they were
struck dumb, and could deny their guilt no more.
And Arion set up, as a thank-offering to the god, an
effigy of a man riding on a dolphin.

Such is the legend given by Herodotus. Another
version makes Apollo appear to Arion in a dream,
assuring him of succour before he leapt overboard,
and adds that, after landing, the bard neglected to
put back again into the sea his preserver, who con-
sequently perished, and was buried by the king of the
country. When the sailors came, they were made to
swear to the truth of their story on the dolphin's tomb,
where Arion had been previously hid. When he suddenly appeared, they confessed their guilt, and were
punished by crucifixion, for the double crime of robbery with intent to murder, and perjury. Arion and
his bearer afterwards became a constellation, by the will
of Apollo, according to a later addition to the legend.

It is not impossible that the legend of Arion grew out
of the group of the man on the dolphin, which may have
been set up to commemorate the expedition which
sailed from Laconia to found Tarentum, comprised of
Dorian and Achæan Greeks; the dolphin, sacred to
Neptune, symbolising the Achæan element, and the
minstrel, loved of Apollo, the Dorian. The legend of
Colston, the munificent Bristol merchant, whose anniver-

sary is still celebrated at Bristol, is well known in the
west of England.   A ship in which he sailed was said
to have sprung a leak, which was miraculously plugged
by a self-sacrificing dolphin, and so the ship came home
safe. Some rationalists have volunteered the prosaic
explanation that Colston was saved and brought home
in another vessel called the Dolphin.   One of the
charitable societies formed in his honour bears the
name of the " Dolphin."   The sacred character of this
fish (or rather cetacean) is doubtless of remote antiquity.   He is the subject of a little poem (exquisite
in the original) by Philip of Thessalonica.

The Dolphin and the Nightingale.

" Blaming Boreas, o'er the sea I was flying slowly,
For the wind of Thrace to me is a thing unholy,
When his back a dolphin showed, bending with devotion,
And the child of æther rode on the child of ocean.
I am that sweet-chanting bird whom the night doth smile
    at ;
And like one that kept his word proved my dolphin pilot.
As he glided onward still with his oarless rowing,
With the lute within my bill I did cheer his going.
Dolphins never ply for hire, but for love and glory,
When the sons of song require ; trust Arion's story."

There is also a beautiful version of the legend by
the Roman poet Ovid.

Cleisthenes of Sicyon was another eminent tyrant,
and a magnificent man in every way. He had one
beautiful daughter named Agariste, through whom despotism was fated to receive its death-blow in Athens.
Like the Orsinis and Colonnas of medieval Rome,

whose feuds gave Rienzi his opportunity to establish democracy, the patrician families of the Isagorids and Alcmæonids strove for supremacy at Athens, and their strife gave birth to freedom. Herodotus gives a quaint account of the foundation of the great wealth of the latter family.

Alcmæon, the son of Megacles, had assisted Crœsus in his negotiations with the Delphic oracle, and was invited in consequence to the court of Sardis. When he had arrived, Crœsus gave him leave to go into the treasury and take as much gold as he could carry away on his person at one time. So he put on the largest tunic he could find, so as to make a capacious fold, and the roomiest buskins. First he stowed his boots with gold dust, then he packed his clothes with it, then he powdered his hair with it, and lastly he took a mouthful of it, and so came out of the treasury " dragging his legs with difficulty, and looking like anything rather than a human being, as his mouth was choked up, and everything about him was in a plethoric state." When Crœsus saw him he was highly amused, and gave him what he had taken and as much again. When Alcmæon came home to Athens he found himself rich enough to enter as a competitor at the great Olympic games, and win the blue ribbon of that national festival—the four-horse chariot-race, which made the winner a hero in the eyes of his countrymen for ever.

Two generations afterwards this family made a splendid marriage. Cleisthenes of Sicyon had added this to his renown, that he too had been a victor at Olympia. Under these circumstances he was not inclined to throw away a beauty and heiress like his

daughter Agariste on the first comer, but, like the
father in Goldoni's "Matrimonio per concorso," he proclaimed that she should be wooed and won by public
competition. He invited all the most eligible youths
in Greece to come and spend a year at his court, pro-
mising to give his decision when it had elapsed; and
he prepared an arena expressly for the purpose of test-
ing their athletic proficiency. Among the suitors was
the exquisite Smyndyrides of Sybaris, the most luxurious man of the most luxurious Hellenic city. It was
he who was said to have complained of the crumpled
rose-leaf on his couch, and to have fainted when he
once saw a man hard at work in the fields. He would
certainly have broken down in the athletic ordeal.
Not so Males, the brother of Titormus, a kind of human gorilla of enormous strength who lived in the
wilds of Ætolia; but he would scarcely have been
polished enough as a son-in-law for Cleisthenes. And
the father might be loath to intrust his daughter to the
son of Pheidon, the despot of Argos, a man notorious
for rapacity and violence. The two Athenian candi-
dates, Megacles son of Alcmæon,* and Hippocleides, a
member of the great rival family, were probably the
favourites from the first; for it is hard to imagine that
there was no betting on an occasion so tempting to
the sporting characters of antiquity. Cleisthenes having
first ascertained that his guests could give satisfactory
references, made proof of their manhood, their tempers,
their accomplishments, and their tastes,—sometimes
bringing them altogether, sometimes holding private

* The son in this family took the grandfather's name : Megacles, Alcmæon, Megacles, Alcmæon, and so on. This was
Alcmæon II.

conversations with each. Although gymnastics were
very important, he seemed to have laid most stress on
their qualities as diners-out. The man who at tho
end of the year seemed, in the opinion of all, to have
the best chance, was Hippocleides, who indeed was
connected with the royal Cypselids of Corinth, as well
as an Athenian of the highest fashion. When the
great day arrived for the suitors to know their fate,
Cleisthenes sacrificed a hundred oxen, and gave a public feast, to which he invited not only the foreign
suitors, but all his own people. After the feast there
was one more trial in music and in rhetoric,—probably
to see how the suitors could carry their wine. As the
cup went round, Hippocleïdes, abashing the rest of the
party by his assurance, called to the flute-player to
strike up a dance. Then he danced, in a manner which
gave perfect satisfaction to himself, though Cleisthenes
began to look grave. Next he ordered a table to be
brought in, mounted on it, and rehearsed certain Laconian and Attic figures. To crown all, he stood on his
head and kicked his legs in the air. This last per-
formance, which Hippocleides might perhaps have
learnt in his youth from the street-boys of the Piræus,
was too much for Cleisthenes, who had long contained
himself with difficulty. "Son of Tisander, thou hast
danced away thy marriage," he exclaimed, in fierce
disgust. The other quietly answered, "Hippocleides
does not care!" from which "Hippocleides don't care"
became a proverbial expression. Then, as Herodotus
tells us, Cleisthenes rose and spoke to this effect:—

"Gentlemen, suitors of my daughter,—I am well
pleased with you all—so well pleased that, if it were possible, I would make you all my sons-in-law. But as I

have but one daughter, that is unfortunately impossible. You have all done me much honour in desiring the alliance of my house. In consideration of this, and of the inconvenience to which you have been put in wasting your valuable time at my court, I beg to present you with a talent of silver each. But to Megacles, the son of Alcmæon, I betroth my daughter Agariste to be his wife according to the usage of Athens."

The issue of this marriage was Cleisthenes, the great Athenian reformer, who was named after his maternal grandfather.

Pisistratus, the despot of Athens, has been already mentioned as contemporary with Crœsus. He won immortality by digesting the poems of Homer into a consecutive whole,—settling, as it were, the canon of the Greek Scriptures. His rule was just and mild, until his enemies forced greater severity upon him in his latter days. He was succeeded by his son Hippias. An abortive attempt to assassinate this prince was made by two men bound together by the tie of romantic friendship peculiar to the Greeks, Harmodius and Aristogeiton. This pair have always been celebrated as model patriots by the admirers of tyrannicide ; but they bungled in their business by slaying the wrong brother, Hipparchus instead of Hippias, and only provoked Hippias to sterner measures of repression. At last the Alcmæonids, growing weary of exile, made such strong interest with the god of Delphi that his oracle continually urged the Spartans to expel the Pisistratids. The clan, after a long struggle, were compelled to quit Athens, and retired to Sigeium, on the Hellespont, having selected this asylum as most convenient for intriguing with the Court of Persia for their restoration. They had ruled in

Athens from B.O. 560 to B.O. 510, which was about the
date of the expulsion of the kings from Rome. They
traced their origin to Codrus and Melanthus, semi-
mythical kings of Attica, and remotely to the Homeric
Nestor of Pylos, after whose son Pisistratus the great
ruler of Athens was named.

A festival song in honour of the famous tyrannicides
was long the " Marseillaise " of republican Athens :—

THE SWORD AND THE MYRTLE.

I'll wreath with myrtle-bough my sword,
Like those who struck down Athens' lord,
Our laws engrafting equal right on—
Harmodius and Aristogeiton.

Harmodius dear, thou art not dead,
But in the happy isles, they say,
Where fleet Achilles lives for aye,
And good Tydeides Diomed.

I'll wreath my sword with myrtle-bough,
Like those who laid Hipparchus low,
When on Athenè's holiday
The tyrant wight they dared to slay.

Because they slew him, and because
They gave to Athens equal laws,
Eternal fame shall shed a light on
Harmodius and Aristogeiton.

CHAPTER VIII.

IONIA.

"O for a tongue to curse the slave,
Whose treason, like a deadly blight,
Comes o'er the counsels of the brave,
And blasts them in their hour of might!"
— MOORE, " Fire-Worshippers."

DARIUS had not forgotten the good service done him by Histiæus of Miletus, in preserving the Danube bridge for him on his hurried retreat from the Scythian expedition. He had given him a grant of land in Thrace, in a most desirable position for a new settlement. But he was afterwards persuaded that he had done wrong. A shrewd Greek would be tempted to form there the nucleus of an independent power. He therefore sent for Histiæus, and detained him in an honourable captivity in his own court at Susa. And this detention led to the great Persian war.

There was a revolution in the little island of Naxos. "The men of substance," as they were literally called, were expelled, and came to Miletus begging Aristagoras, now deputy - governor in the absence of his father-in-law Histiæus, to restore them. Thinking to get Naxos for himself, Aristagoras procured the aid of

a Persian flotilla. On the way, a quarrel arose about
a Greek captain whom Megabates, the Persian admiral,
had punished, because he found no watch set on board
his ship. The punishment consisted in binding him
down so that his head protruded from one of the ports
or rowlocks, and Aristagoras had taken upon himself
to release him. Megabates, in dudgeon, sent to warn
the Naxians, who were to have been surprised, and the
expedition failed. Then Aristagoras, finding himself
unable to pay the expenses of the armament, as had
been stipulated, thought of securing his position by
the desperate expedient of stirring up a revolt at
Miletus against Persia. He was confirmed in this
resolution by the arrival of a singular courier from
Histiæus, who was determined at any cost to escape
from the forced hospitalities of Susa. Histiæus had
taken a slave, shaved his head, punctured certain letters
on the bare crown, then kept him till the hair was
grown, and sent him to Aristagoras with merely the ,
verbal message that he was to shave his head. When
Aristagoras had played the barber, he found that the
living despatch bore the word "revolt."

His first step was to proclaim democracy throughout
the Greek confederacy. The different despots were
given up to their fellow-citizens, to be dealt with according to their deserts. It speaks strongly in favour
of the character of their "tyranny," that nearly all
were dismissed uninjured. One only—Coes of Mytilene
—was stoned to death. Aristagoras then set sail for
Sparta to seek for aid. That state at this time enjoyed the singular constitution of a double monarchy.
This may have had some mythological connection
with the legend of the twin sons of Leda, Castor and

Pollux, who became sea-gods, from whom the constellation of the Gemini was named; but Herodotus assigns to it a different origin.

His tradition is that when the sons of Hercules reconquered their heritage of the Peloponnese, one of their three chiefs, Aristodemus, had the kingdom of Sparta for his share. His wife gave birth to twins just before his death. The boys were much alike; and the mother, hoping that they might both be kings, protested that she did not know them apart. The Spartans were puzzled; and the Delphic oracle gave an answer which hardly mended the matter, except so far that it satisfied the mother.

"Let both be kings, but let the elder have more honour."

But which was the elder? that was the question. At last it was suggested that a watch should be set to see which the mother washed and fed first. If she acted on system, the case was clear. The espionage succeeded; the elder was discovered, and named Eurysthenes, and the other Procles. The two brothers, when they grew up, were said to have been always at variance, and their separate lines continued so ever after. The two kings had peculiar duties, rights, and privileges, but lived in the same plain way as other citizens.

When Aristagoras arrived at Sparta, he was admitted to an audience with the senior king, Cleomenes. He showed him a bronze tablet engraved with a chart—the earliest known map of the world—pointed out where all the different nations lay, and conjured him to assist his kinsmen the Ionians; observing, that it was foolish

for the Spartans to fritter away their force in local
feuds, when they might be lords of Asia. As for the
Persians, they were an easy prey—men who actually
" went into battle with trousers on." Cleomenes promised to give him an answer in three days. At the
second interview he asked "how far it was to Susa?"
Aristagoras was unguarded enough to say, "a three
months' journey;" on which Cleomenes ordered him
to quit Sparta before sunset. Then he returned and
sat before the king in the sacred guise of a suppliant,
with an olive-bough in his hand. A little daughter of
Cleomenes, named Gorgo, aged eight or nine, was
standing at her father's side. The Milesian wished
her to be sent away, but Cleomenes told him to say
on, and not to heed the child. Then Aristagoras began by offering ten talents, and as the king shook his
head, increased them by degrees to fifty. When this
sum was mentioned, the child cried out, " Go away,
father, or the strange man will be sure to bribe thee." *
The "conscience of the king" was moved. He withdrew to escape the temptation, and the mission of
Aristagoras failed at Sparta.

At Athens he had better chances of success. Athens
was in the heyday of her first freedom. She had rid
herself of her Tyrants, the Pisistratids, who were at

---

* Gorgo was well worthy to become, as she afterwards did,
the wife of Leonidas. An incident in her married life, subsequently related by Herodotus, seems to militate against the
dictum of Aristotle that the Spartan women were inferior to
the men. All the authorities of Sparta were puzzled by the
arrival of a waxen tablet (the usual form of a despatch) with
nothing written on it. When Gorgo heard of it, she at once
suggested that the wax should be scraped off, and the despatch
was found engraven on the wood.

this moment intriguing with Persia, not without success, for their restoration. The feelings of the citizens
towards these powerful absentees and their Asiatic
friends were much the same as those of the French of
1792 towards the Emigration and its abettors. The
two great ruling families were now the rival houses of
Alcmæon and Isagoras. Cleisthenes the Alcmæonid,
grandson of the tyrant of Sicyon, might not have
thought it worth his while to court the people, had he
not been determined to put down the rival faction
which was led by Isagoras, brother of his father's rival
Hippocleides, of dancing notoriety. As it was, he
brought about a complete democratic revolution. He
broke up the four old tribes, which were bound by
family ties and sacred rites, and made ten new geographical divisions. This was as radical a change as the
substitution of departments for provinces in France;
and the introduction of the decimal system, in nearly
every department of state at Athens, anticipated by
more than two thousand years the work of the French
Revolution. The Isagorids for a time turned the
tables on the Alcmæonids, by calling in the assistance
of the Spartans, and Cleisthenes had only just defeated
a dangerous confederacy against Athens. The Spartans
had invaded Attica from Megara, when the Bœotians
and Chalcidians broke in upon their northern frontier.
But the usual jealousy between the two Spartan kings,
and the defection of their Corinthian allies, dissolved
the Spartan army, and left the Athenians at leisure
to deal with their other enemies. They defeated
the Bœotians with great slaughter, taking seven hundred prisoners; and crossing on the same day to Eubœa,
there obtained a second victory over the Chalcidians, in

whose lands they afterwards planted a military colony. The prisoners were ransomed, but their chains still hung in the citadel of Athens in the time of Herodotus on the walls blackened with Persian fire, and a handsome bronze quadriga stood by the gateway, which had been offered to Minerva from the tithe of the ransom. Its inscription was to this effect :—

" Armies of nations twain, Bœotia banded with Chalcis,
  Sons of Athenian sires quelled in the labour of war,
 Slaking their ardent pride in a dismal fetter of iron—
  Then to the Maid for tithe gave we the chariot-and-
   four."

The energy of Athens at this time struck Herodotus forcibly. It was like that of the French Jacobins when they had enemies on every frontier, and the Vendée and the Federals of the South on their hands besides. Great political changes give a nation a present sense of life and happiness, which is too often ultimately wrecked by selfishness, but which seems for a time to inspire superhuman strength. The worsted Thebans stirred up the little island of Ægina, which was always a thorn in the side of Athens till she had become mistress of the sea. There was a very old-standing feud about some sacred images or fetishes of olive-wood, representing the goddess Ceres and her daughter Persephone. No doubt their holiness was enhanced by their age and ugliness. Artistic beauty seems to have little to do with the sacredness of images, and in modern times in Italy an old black Madonna has been an object of peculiar veneration. The Zeus of Phidias and the Aphrodite of Praxiteles were not moulded by the hands of Faith.

The Athenians had just refused a demand of the

Persian satrap of Sardis for the restoration of their tyrant Hippias, when Aristagoras arrived. They received him with open arms, not only on account of this, but also because Miletus was their own colony; and despatched twenty ships—probably all they could spare from the Æginetan war—to aid the Milesians in their struggle against the yoke of Persia. These were joined by five galleys from Eretria in Eubœa, that city being under an obligation to the Milesians. The crews left their ships on the shore near Ephesus, and marched on and surprised Sardis, shutting up the Persians in the citadel. But Sardis proved to them a miniature Moscow. The town, mainly built of wood and reeds, caught fire, and the buccaneers thought it best to retreat as soon as a sack became out of the question. But the Persian forces caught them up near Ephesus, and inflicted severe punishment before they could reach their ships. The Ionian Greeks were now left to themselves by the Athenians, but the insurrection assumed large proportions, involving the whole Greek seaboard of Asia, many inland tribes, and lastly spreading to the island of Cyprus.

When Darius heard of the great revolt, and especially of the burning of Sardis, his wrath was greatly kindled against the Athenians. He took a bow and shot towards heaven, saying, "O Zeus! grant that I may be avenged on the Athenians!" He also appointed a slave to say to him thrice every day during dinner, "O king! remember the Athenians."* Then he sent

---

* There is a parallel symbolism in the case of Elisha and Joash (2 Kings xiii. 17): "Then Elisha said, Shoot; and he shot. And he said, The arrow of the Lord's deliverance, and the arrow of deliverance from Syria."

for Histiæus, telling him that he suspected he knew
something about the business. But the Greek's innocent
look and plausible words deceived the king, who was
induced to send him to the coast—the very thing he
had desired—to help to quell the insurrection. At
Sardis Histiæus found an astuter head to deal with.
The satrap there was Artaphernes the king's brother.
He said, "I see how it is, Histiæus—thou hast stitched
the shoe, and Aristagoras has put it on." But the
adroit Ionian managed for the time to escape out of
all his difficulties. He even outwitted Artaphernes so
far, that, as Mr Grote supposes, he got him to execute
a number of innocent Persians at Sardis, by opening a
treasonable correspondence with them. The Milesians,
however, would not receive him back as governor :
he therefore persuaded the Lesbians to give him eight
triremes, with which he took to piracy on his own account in the parts about the Hellespont. While ma-
rauding on the coast near Lesbos, he was defeated by
a Persian force which happened to be there, and his
captors, fearing lest the good-natured Darius might pardon him, put him to death at Sardis. Their fears were
well founded; for when they sent his head to the king,
Darius expressed much regret, and ordered it to be
buried with all honour. This is quite consistent with
the character of the Persian king as drawn by the
prophet Daniel. It seems as if no one who had once
done him a service could ever afterwards forfeit his
good graces.

After reducing Cyprus, the Persians fell with their
combined force on the Ionians and their allies. A victory won by the Greek fleet over the Phœnician sailors
of Darius had no result of importance. The Carians

fought most valiantly, and cut off a whole Persian
division by an ambuscade. Though they lost in one
battle ten thousand men, yet their spirit was unbroken.
Miletus, too, still held out gallantly. If any man under these circumstances ought to have shown an example of self-devotion, that man was Aristagoras.
But nerve is inconsistent with levity of character. It
often happens that the coward runs into the jaws of
his fate, and so it happened to him. He abandoned the
Ionian cause, and with some of his partisans sailed away
for his father-in-law's new settlement in Thrace, where
he was killed while besieging some petty town. He had
been just in time to make his fruitless escape, for the
Persians now proceeded to invest Miletus by land and
sea. The allied Greeks decided on leaving it to defend
itself by land, and concentrating their fleet at a small
island off the coast. The allies counted in all three
hundred and fifty triremes, which were confronted by
six hundred in the service of Persia. The Persian commanders first tried to dissolve the hostile confedera-
tion by sending the deposed despots each to their own
countrymen with promises of pardon on submission, and
threats of extermination in case of prolonged resistance.
The plan so far failed that it did not supersede the necessity of an action, for each separate state imagined itself the only one to which overtures were made. The
Ionian captains, in their council of war, now agreed to
put themselves all under the command of Dionysius
of Phocæa. He set to work to put the ships in constant training, especially practising a manœuvre something like that of Nelson, — attacking the enemy's
line in columns, and cutting through it. The invention of steam-rams seems likely to make the sea-fights

of the future more like those of the remote past than
ever. The incidents of the Merrimac's battle and of
Lissa recall the collisions of ancient navies, only that
the oars of the galleys are superseded by steam-engines.
Their sails were not used in action, as they would have
only embarrassed the rowers. To sweep away a whole
broadside of oars by cleverly shaving the enemy, and
then turn sharply and ram him home on the quarter,
was doubtless a favourite evolution of the best sailors.
Dionysius was too much of a martinet for the self-in-
dulgent Ionians. He kept them at sea all night—an
unheard-of innovation—and at drill all day, and the
days were terribly hot. They had not bargained for
this when they chose him admiral. They began to
murmur. "What god have we offended that we should
be thus victimised? What fools we were to give ourselves up body and soul to this Phocæan bully, who
commands but three ships of his own! We shall fall
sick with the work and heat. The Persians can but
make us slaves, and no slavery can well be worse than
this. Let us mutiny." So they landed and encamped
on the island, lolled in the shade all day, and refused
to go on board any more. Then the Persian poison
began to work. Æaces, the son of Syloson, lately
tyrant of Samos, succeeded in persuading his countrymen to promise to desert, and they alone had sixty
ships. Little could be hoped now from a general
battle, but the battle took place. The Samians went
off, all but eleven ships, whose stanch captains, like
Nelson at Copenhagen with his blind eye to the telescope, would not see the signal of retreat. Most of the
other allied squadrons, when they saw what the Samians
were doing, imitated their bad example. The Chian

contingent, with the Samian eleven and a few others,
maintained a desperate struggle. The hundred Chian
ships, each with forty picked marines on board, charged
repeatedly through the enemy's line. When they had
taken many of his galleys, and lost half their own, such
as were able made their way to their own island. Their
damaged ships made for Mycalè, where the crews ran
them ashore and marched to Ephesus. But ill fortune
followed them. It was night, and the Ephesians were
celebrating a feast, whose chief ceremony was a torch-
light procession of women.   Thinking them a party.
of freebooters come to carry off their wives and
daughters, the citizens sallied out and cut them all to
pieces. Dionysius the Phocæan had taken three ships,
thus exactly doubling his own number. When he saw
that the fight was lost, he made straight for the coast
of Phœnicia, left undefended by the absence of their
war-galleys, sank a number of merchantmen in the
harbours, and gained by this booty the means of setting up handsomely as a corsair in Sicily, where he
plundered Carthaginians and Tyrrhenians, but—with
" a refinement of delicacy very unusual," as Mr Rawlinson observes—let all Greek vessels go free.

The fall of Miletus soon followed the sea-fight. Most
of the men were killed, and the women and children
enslaved. The Athenians were deeply affected by the
news, and when their poet Phrynichus brought on the
stage his tragedy of the "Capture of Miletus," the
audience burst into tears, and he was fined a thousand
drachmas (francs), and forbidden ever to exhibit it
again. The revolt, which had now been desperately
maintained for six years, was terribly expiated. The
towns on the coast were as far as possible depopulated

(the people being sent to the interior) ; and the islands
were traversed by lines of soldiers, who "netted" the
inhabitants from one side to the other. Cities
and temples were burnt to the ground. The Chians
had been warned of coming evil by terrible portents.
Of a hundred youths sent to Delphi, all but two had
died of a pestilence ; and just before the great sea-fight
off Miletus, the roof of a public school had fallen on
the heads of the children of the principal citizens, and
only one had escaped out of a hundred and twenty.
In 1821 Europe was roused to sympathy for Greece
by the horrors which this very island (Scio) suffered
from the troops of the Capudan Pasha.

After a time the policy of the Persians changed towards Ionia, probably because Darius disapproved of the
excessive severity which had been exercised ; and Mardonius, his son-in-law, a young noble of great promise,
was sent to depose once more the "tyrants," and establish democracies. These rulers had proved that they
were not to be trusted. Having settled this business
to the king's satisfaction, he was appointed to the
command of a fleet and army whose destination was
Athens and Eretria—for Darius had never forgotten
their offence in the burning of Sardis. But the ulterior
object of the expedition was the subjugation of all
Greece.

As the Persian fleet was doubling Mount Athos,
a north wind sprang up which terribly shattered it.
Little short of three hundred wrecks and twenty
thousand corpses were cast away on the rocky promontory. Many fell victims, says Herodotus, to sea-
monsters—one of the additional perils of the deep in
the imagination of ancient mariners ; those who could

not swim were drowned—and those who could, died
of cold.   Mardonius himself received a wound in
an action on the mainland of Thrace, and the
expedition returned home with its commander in-
valided.   Darius immediately made fresh preparations, and sent heralds to all the Greek states to demand earth and water, in order that he might know
what support to expect.   It is to be hoped that
the Athenians and Spartans did not disgrace themselves by throwing one of the heralds into a well and
the other into a pit, and telling them to fetch earth
and water thence; but such is the story.   Darius
himself would under no provocation have so forgotten
his knighthood.   Some years afterwards, the Spartans
were said to have sent two of their citizens, who
voluntarily offered themselves, to Susa, as an atonement for this outrage, for which they believed that
the wrath of the hero Talthybius, the patron of
heralds, lay heavy on them; but Xerxes, who was
then king, would not accept the sacrifice, and dismissed
them unhurt.

The Æginetans gave the earth and water to Darius,
probably to spite the Athenians, who at once denounced
them to the Spartans (who were as yet considered
the leaders of Greece) as traitors to the national cause.
The Spartan king Cleomenes went to Ægina to arrest
the most guilty parties; but his mission there was
foiled by his brother-king Demaratus, who was accusing
him at home.   In retaliation, Cleomenes attempted to
prove that Demaratus was illegitimate.   His mother
was the loveliest woman in Sparta.   She had been
ugly in her childhood, but was changed into a beauty
by her nurse taking her daily to the temple of Helen.

There a mysterious lady—"tall as the gods, and most divinely fair"—one day laid her hand on the child, whose looks from that time forth began to amend. In due time she had been married to a noble Spartan; but Ariston the king fell in love with her, and got her from her husband, who was his greatest friend, by a ruse. He proposed to exchange their most precious possessions, and they ratified the compact by an oath. Ariston straightway demanded his friend's wife. Thus taken off his guard, and bound by his oath, the husband unwillingly resigned her. But from circumstances connected with the birth of the child Demaratus, he was supposed by some to be not the son of Ariston, but of her former husband. Cleomenes found a powerful ally in Leotychides, the next heir, who was a deadly enemy of Demaratus, and the suit was carried on in his name. The inevitable oracle of Delphi was the last court of appeal; and the priestess, being bribed by Cleomenes, pronounced against Demaratus, who was then deposed, and ultimately driven from Sparta by the taunts of Leotychides. He made his way to that paradise of refugees, the hospitable court of Darius, who gave him lands and cities. He had stood very high in the estimation of his countrymen, as having been the only Spartan who had won the four-horse chariot-race at Olympia.

When Cleomenes had thus worked his will on Demaratus, he took Leotychides, his new associate on the throne, with him to Ægina, where he arrested two of the principal citizens, as guilty of treason against the liberty of Greece, and deposited them as hostages with their bitter enemies the Athenians. But his own end was near. Rumour accused him of underhand practices against Demaratus, and he fled into Arcadia, where he began to hatch a conspiracy against Sparta. The Spartans in alarm called him home to his former honours. He had always been eccentric; he now became a maniac. He would dash his staff in the face of every citizen he met. At last his friends put him in the stocks—a wholesome instrument of restraint, as common there as in our own country within the last century. Finding himself alone one day with his keeper, he asked for a knife. The Helot did not dare to refuse the king, though a prisoner. Then he committed suicide in a manner which, though effected more clumsily, resembled the "Happy Despatch" of the Japanese.

The madness of Cleomenes, like that of Cambyses, was generally supposed to have been a judgment on his impiety. Herodotus thought his treatment of Demaratus enough to account for it; but other charges equally grave were brought against him. He had bribed the Pythian priestess. He had roasted alive some fifty Argives who had taken refuge in a sacred grove, during his invasion of Argolis, by burning the grove itself. He had scourged Argive priests for not allowing him, a foreigner, to sacrifice in the temple of Juno. He had been in the habit of entering forbidden temples, and generally of making a parade of reckless irreligion. The Spartans themselves, however, gave a more naturalistic account of the cause of his madness. Certain Scythian ambassadors, who were staying at Sparta to negotiate a league against Darius, had induced the king to adopt the habit of taking his wine without water like themselves. "To drink like a Scythian" was a proverb. The case of Cambyses, as we have seen, admitted of the like explanation.

When Cleomenes was dead, the Æginetans sent to
Sparta to complain of Leotychides about their hostages,
who were still in custody with the Athenians.   Leotychides, who was not popular, narrowly escaped being
given up as a hostage in their stead; but, in the end,
he was duly sent to Athens to demand their release.
The Athenians refused to give them up, saying that
as two kings had placed them there, they could not
give them up to one.   They certainly would have had
the English law of trusteeship on their side.   Leotychides, however, read them a striking lesson on the
sacredness of trusts.   He told them how one Glaucus,
a Spartan, had once consulted the oracle at Delphi as
to restoring a deposit of money to its rightful owner.
He had the audacity to ask whether he might venture
to purge himself by an oath, according to the Greek
law, and so keep the money.   The Pythoness gave
answer in these warning words :—

> " O Glaucus, gold is good to win,
>   And a false oath is easy sin ;
>   Swear—an thou wilt : death follows both
>   The righteous and unrighteous oath :
>   But Perjury breeds an awful Birth,
>   That hath no name in heaven or earth ;
>   Strong without hands, swift without feet,
>   It tracks the pathway of deceit—
>   Sweeps its whole household from the land ;
>   Only the just man's house shall stand."

When Glaucus heard these words, he at once restored
the money, and sent to beg of the god that the thought
of his heart might be forgiven him.   The oracle replied that to tempt heaven with such a question was
as bad as to commit the sin.   "And now," said the

Spartan king, "mark my words, men of Athens; at this day there is none of Glaucus' race left in Sparta :· they have perished, root and branch."

The Athenians, however, turned a deaf ear to the solemn monition. In return for their stubbornness, the Æginetans laid wait for and captured the Sacred Galley which carried the Athenian embassy to Delos periodically, and threw the envoys (men of the highest rank) into prison. A fierce war of reprisals was entered upon, of which perhaps the most remarkable characteristic is the poverty of the Athenians of the period in ships. They were obliged to beg twenty galleys of their friends the Corinthians, who, as it was against the law to give them, generously sold the whole for a hundred drachmæ—about five francs apiece.

Leotychides might have served to point the moral of his own remarkable anecdote. He reaped little happiness from the successful plot by which he had supplanted Demaratus. After seeing his only son die before him, he ended his own days in exile, having been banished from Sparta for the disgraceful crime of taking bribes from the enemy during a war with the Thessalians. The evident satisfaction with which Herodotus, here as elsewhere, traces the course of retributive justice, is highly characteristic of the historian.

CHAPTER IX.

MARATHON.

" The flying Mede, his shaftless broken bow !
The fiery Greek, his red pursuing spear !
Mountains above, Earth's, Ocean's plain below !
Such was the scene."
—BYRON, "Childe Harold."

As the first expedition against Greece under Mardonius had ended in disaster, Darius thought it best to let the young commander gain experience before he was intrusted with the conduct of another ; possibly, also, his wound was long in healing. The second armada was put under the command of Datis, a Mede of mature years, and Artaphernes, nephew of the king. They had express orders to bring the Athenians and Eretrians into the royal presence in chains. The whole flotilla —six hundred war-ships, besides transports—struck straight across sea, through the Archipelago, not caring again to tempt the dangers of Athos. After sacking Naxos, they came to the sacred island of Delos, the birthplace of the twin deities Apollo and Diana. Fortunately for the inhabitants, the senior commander was a Median ritualist, not an iconoclast like Cambyses, and the sacred island was more than spared.

Herodotus mentions an earthquake as occurring soon after this visit, and Thucydides another; and the story of the island having once floated about at large, before it became fixed, is doubtless connected with its volcanic origin. The Persian armament swept like a blight through the other islands, and soon appeared off the coast of Euboea. Meeting with no resistance on landing, they disembarked their cavalry, and laid siege to Eretria, which was betrayed to them after six days of severe fighting. The town was burnt and sacked, and the inhabitants carried away captive. They expected from the threats of Darius the worst of fates; but when they reached Susa, that forgiving monarch settled them peaceably at a place called Ardericca, where there was a famous well which produced salt, bitumen, and petroleum. Herodotus saw them there, and mentions particularly that they had not forgotten their Greek.

The Athenians, after the fall of Eretria, must have felt much as the Jews did when Sennacherib appeared before their walls, and Rabshakeh boasted that all the kings 'and gods on his march had fallen before him. But when they heard that the Persians had actually disembarked at Marathon, they must have felt as England would have felt had the news come that Buonaparte had landed in Pevensey Bay, close to the ominous field of Hastings. For Marathon had not as yet become a synonym for Victory; on the contrary, Pisistratus had beaten the Athenian commons on that plain, and his son Hippias was now with the Persian host in a temper which, they might be sure, had not improved with old age, exile, and disappointment.

It was Hippias who, from old association, and thinking the plain well suited for cavalry manœuvres, had guided the Persians to the strand of Marathon (now Vrana). The plain itself is shaped somewhat like a thin crescent, the sea washing its concavity, and mountains rising behind its convex rim, which opens out at the back into two valleys. Between both a spur runs out, commanding the two gaps. The slope of this spur was the key of the Athenian position. The extent of level ground is about six miles long, as measured by the curve of the bay, and about a mile and a half broad. But although along the whole of the six miles there is a fine sandy beach for landing, behind it, a considerable part—more than a third—of the crescent-plain is occupied by two swamps, one of which is of considerable extent. Here the Persian army awaited the mustering of the Athenians. Why they did not push on at once into the country is a mystery.

It so chanced that, just before the Persians came, a heaven-sent commander dropped, as it were, from the clouds into the fortunate city of Athens. The spirits of men rose when it was rumoured that Miltiades, the son of Cimon, had come home. Herodotus gives us his family history, which was curious enough.

The Chersonese is a tongue of land jutting into the sea from the Thracian mainland. Its people being annoyed by the incursions of some savages to the north, as the Britons were by the Picts and Scots, sent a deputation to the oracle at Delphi to ask for advice. The god told them to choose as king the first man who should welcome them to his house. For some time they traversed almost hopelessly various parts of Greece; but Greek respectability was not likely to invite into its sanctuary a party of strangers "dressed in outlandish garments, and carrying long spears in their hands." At last in Attica they passed by the countryhouse of one Miltiades, son of Cypselus (a descendant of the hero of the "meal-bin").* The democratic Tyranny had deprived him of occupation, for he was a nobleman of the old school, who came of "a four-horse family," says our historian—had won, indeed, the great Olympic race himself—who traced his pedigree back to Ajax, and was connected with the proud Isagorids. So he sat idle in his porch, heartily sick of Pisistratus and democratic respectability. Seeing the foreign wayfarers pass, out of mere curiosity, as it would seem, he invited them into his house and entertained them. The interview was satisfactory; Miltiades consented to take out a few colonists with them to their wilds, and be their king. The first thing he did was to build them a kind of Hadrian's wall to keep back their Picts and Scots. His nephew, Stesagoras, the son of Cimon, succeeded him, and was succeeded, on his violent death, by his brother, this second Miltiades, who came out from Athens, and made himself by a *coup d'état* despot of the whole Chersonese—a great sin in the eyes of his democratic countrymen, who brought him to trial for it when he came to Athens, but condoned it on account of his services to the state. When the Persians, in their march of vengeance after the Ionian revolt, came to the Hellespont, he ran the gauntlet of their fleet successfully with five galleys; but he left in their hands one ship, on board of which was his son. As Miltiades had advised the king's bridge

* See p. 103.

over the Danube to be destroyed, his captors thought, when they sent the youth to Darius, that he would punish the father in his person; but, with his usual magnanimity, the king gave him a house and estate, and a Persian wife, by whom he became the founder of a Persian family.

Miltiades, immediately on his return to Athens, was impeached by his democratic enemies for "tyranny" in his colony; but, having cleared his character, he was at once appointed one of the ten Athenian generals, of whom Callimachus, the polemarch, or minister of war, was another. They could not have been much more than colonels, except on the days when they held the command in rotation; an arrangement which, to our English notions, would be fatal to the success of any great enterprise. The Athenians were as fond of decimals as the Persians of the number seven. A traditional 10,000 Athenians were engaged on the Greek side at Marathon. But the Greeks were apt to under-estimate their own numbers and exaggerate those of the enemy. Supposing the Persian force to amount in all to 200,000 men, making deductions for the guard of the ships and the absent cavalry, they probably brought not many more than 110,000 into the field, of whom 30,000 were heavy armed. The Athenian light armed must also be reckoned, and if their whole force is put at 18,000, with 2000 Platæans, the odds still leave abundant room for Hellenic self-glorification. Before the Athenians left their city, they had sent to Sparta for succour. Their courier is said to have reached Sparta on foot—a distance of 140 English miles—on the second day. But the Spartans had an inveterate superstition against marching until the

moon was full. They were possibly in no great hurry
to help Athens, as, when they did come, it was too
late, and only with two thousand men. The Athenians had already drawn up their line of battle in the
sacred close of Hercules, at Marathon, when they were
joined by the Platæans. The Platæans had suffered
much in time past from their neighbours the Thebans,
and in return for substantial protection had bound
themselves to Athens; in fact the little state became
a satellite of the greater.

The Greek forces seem to have occupied the space
between Mount Kotroni and Argaliki, resting their
wings against the heights, which prevented their being
outflanked. There was hesitation as to beginning
the attack. On the one hand, the Athenians rested
on their own supplies, and could take their time;
and the Spartan contingent, though tardy, might be
expected to march in six days, when the moon would
be at the full. On the other hand, treachery was
feared from the party of Hippias in Athens, if
there was any delay. The generals were equally
divided, but Miltiades was for immediate action, and
persuaded Callimachus to give his casting-vote with
him. By what arrangement it happened is not
clear, but it is certain that when the day for action
came, the command was in the hands of Miltiades.
Why the attack was made on the particular day it is
difficult to determine. Some suppose that Miltiades,
with an inspiration like that of Wellington at Sala-
manca, saw his advantage in a temporary absence
of the Persian cavalry. Certain it is that no cavalry
are heard of in the action, which seems singular, as
Hippias is said to have chosen the spot for their bene-

fit.* The armies stood fronting each other. Callimachus was on the right wing, and the Platæans on the left.
The right was always the post of honour and of danger,
because the last man had his side unprotected by a shield.
When the Greek line was formed, it appeared too short
as compared with that of the Persians; so Miltiades,
no doubt with some misgivings, drew troops from his
centre and massed them on the wings, in order that
they might deploy when they came into the open.
There was nearly a mile of ground to be cleared before
arriving at the enemy's line; and it was advisable
to lose as few men as possible from arrows before
coming to the thrust of spears. Miltiades therefore
gave the signal to charge at quick step, which was
increased to a run when within range. The Persians,
on their side, prepared to give them a warm reception, though they thought the Greeks mad for charging so wildly, unsupported by archers or cavalry. But
they had scarcely time for admiration of their enemies
before they were in upon them. The two armies
wrestled long and desperately before advantage declared itself for either. At last the swaying line of
combat parted into three fragments, which moved in
different directions. In the centre, where the Persians
and Sacæ were posted, the Athenians were rolled back,
probably no farther than the slope of Kotroni, where
they could stand at bay, though Herodotus says they
were pursued up the valley. On the wings they were

---

* Mr Blakesley thinks that they had not yet been disembarked, but were still at Eretria; and perhaps it was for this
reason that the Persians kept their position close to the shore
for so long a time, and did not attempt to outflank by the hills
an enemy numerically so inferior.

victorious; and the allies of the Persians who were there, retiring creditably enough, with their faces to the enemy, did not see the marshes behind them, but floundered into them backwards. There was struggling to regain a footing, and general confusion, of which the Greeks took advantage, and pressed them harder till they were hopelessly broken and discomfited. But the victorious wings now perceived that their own centre was dislocated from them, and had lost ground before the *élite* of the Persian army; they therefore faced about and fell on their flanks. The Persian centre, now engaged on three sides, at last gave way likewise, and fell back in the direction of their galleys. Covered probably by the archers from the decks, most of the troops got safe on board. Then the Greeks raised a yell of disappointment, called for fire to burn the ships, and many rushed into the water to try to board them. One of the foremost of these was Cynegeirus, brother to the poet Æschylus; but as he grasped the ·stern-ornament of a trireme, he dropt back with both his hands chopped off. Some say that he maintained his hold until he lost first one hand, then the other, and lastly his head, as he caught the gunwale with his teeth.

So ended the immortal battle of Marathon, which stands almost alone by the side of Morgarten among the miracles achieved by the inspiration of Freedom. The Persians were sufficiently beaten, but their rout could hardly have been so complete as Herodotus describes, since they had not far to run. They lost six thousand four hundred men, mostly in the swamps, and seven galleys, held back by main force or carried by boarding. It was in the fight at the ships that, besides

Cynegeirus, many Athenians of note fell, amongst them two of the generals, one of whom was Callimachus. The Athenians lost one hundred and ninety-two men in the action. As the greater number are said to have fallen in the attack on the ships, either those who gave way before the Persians and Sacæ were few, or they only suffered a partial repulse. Greek armies, from their formation in compact phalanx, seldom lost many men until they were broken, when their long spears and heavy armament rendered them more defenceless than lighter troops. Marathon afterwards became a household word at Athens, as Waterloo with us. A "man who had fought at Marathon" had a patent of popular nobility. Athenian orators made it a favourite commonplace; and Athenian satirists found it an inexhaustible fund of jest upon the national vanity. Wonderful stories were related in connection with the battle. On the return of Pheidippides the courier from Sparta, he said that as he was crossing a mountain in Arcadia he was accosted by the wood-god Pan, who called to him by name, and complained of his worship being neglected by the Athenians, while he was always well disposed towards them. In consequence, a temple was dedicated to Pan under the Acropolis, and he was honoured with annual sacrifices and a torch-race. National heroes were supposed to have been present, and to have assisted in the fight; and one Athenian was suddenly struck blind in the thick of the fray by (as he declared) the passing before his eyes of a supernatural giant, who slew the man at his side.

When the Persians had re-embarked, their fleet doubled Cape Sunium, and made a demonstration in the direction of the harbour of Athens, with the hope

of surprising the city ; but the Athenians returned in
time to cover it. There was an ugly rumour, which
Herodotus entirely disbelieves, that a shield was hoisted
on the walls as a telegraphic signal by the Alcmæonids.
This, doubtless, emanated from the opposite faction ;
for the Isagorids and Alcmæonids of Athens hated
each other as cordially, and slandered each other as
unscrupulously, as the English Tories and Whigs of
the time of Queen Anne.

The tale of the subsequent fate of Miltiades is one
of the most painful passages in history. In the first
flush of his popularity, he asked the Athenians to give
him seventy ships fully equipped, only deigning to
tell them that he would get them gold in abundance.
They asked no questions, but gave him the fleet. He
had a private grudge against the people of Paros, and
he now sailed to the island of marble, and laid siege to
its town. His patience began to be at an end, when
a certain priestess offered to forward his views. In
leaping the wall of the sacred precincts after an interview with her, he dislocated his thigh. He then
returned to Athens disabled, and as soon as he arrived
was put upon his trial on the capital charge of having
deceived the state, his accuser being Xanthippus,
father of the great Pericles. The crippled hero lay
on a couch in court while his friends defended him.
They could not say a word in extenuation of the
Parian escapade, but rested his defence on the fact
that he had saved Athens at Marathon, and regained
Lemnos. But, unfortunately for Miltiades, this was
not the first time that he had had to appear on a charge
of like nature. It seemed as if he wished to make
himself despot of Paros — perhaps even despot of

Athens—as he had made himself despot of the Chersonese. It was not for this that they had got rid of
Hippias. If he commanded well at Marathon, so did
the other generals, two of them now no more; nay,
every man who fought in those ranks seemed as good a
hero as he, for Marathon, like Inkermann, was a "soldier's battle." If he took Lemnos, he had missed taking
Paros, and wasted the public money at a time when the
treasury was low. They had not the heart to condemn
him to death, for as he lay before them he seemed to
bear death's mark already—and, indeed, it must have
appeared to them as impossible as for the king of Italy
to punish Garibaldi for treason after his wound at
Aspromonte; but they condemned him in the expenses
of the abortive expedition, amounting to fifty talents
(above £12,000). As his son Cimon was able to pay
these heavy damages, his judges seem to have had no
intention of absolutely ruining him. Soon afterwards,
physical mortification in the injured limb, assisted no
doubt by mental, put an untimely end to the days of
the Man of Marathon.

CHAPTER X.

"Singing of men that in battle array,
  Ready in heart and ready in hand,
  March with banner, and bugle, and fife,
  To the death, for their native land."
          —TENNYSON, "Maud."

AFTER the terrible defeat of his best generals at Marathon, Darius thought the Athenians worth his personal
attention. That battle took place in the autumn of
B.C. 490; and the king occupied the next three years
in preparations for a new expedition, which he intended to lead in person. But a revolt in Egypt divided
his attention; and he was considering in which direction he was most wanted, when he was summoned
from the scene by a mightier monarch than himself,
after a reign of six-and-thirty years. His fourth son,
Xerxes, succeeded him—not his first-born, Artabazanes;
because Xerxes had been born in the purple, and of a
daughter of Cyrus; whereas the elder sons had been
born when Darius was a subject, and of the daughter
of a subject. Xerxes soon disposed of the Egyptian
revolt, and left his brother Achæmenes satrap of the
country. Then he took up the great quarrel bequeathed

him by his father, but after many hesitations and
vacillations, signified in the narrative of Herodotus
by dreams and their interpretations, and opposite
opinions said to have been given by Artabanus,
who dissuaded, and Mardonius, who was in favour
of an invasion. The young king was evidently
afraid of compromising his newly-inherited prosperity. He was of a luxurious character, not crav-
ing, like Darius, for barren honour; and if he left
the Greeks alone, it would be a long time before they
found their way to Susa. When the bolder counsels
at last prevailed, he resolved to make matters as safe
as possible. Grecian liberty was not to be stabbed,
but stifled, to death. He would pour out all Asia upon
it. So he took four good years in preparation, gather-
ing a host of armed, half-armed, and almost unarmed
men, such as has hardly been seen before or since. The
soldiers, with the exception of the select few, carried
the rudest national weapons—bows and arrows, pole-
axes, "morning-stars," even staves and lassoes. Some
rate the host as high as five millions; others give less
than half that number. The men were measured, like
dry goods—not counted; that is, a pen was made
which could hold ten thousand, through which the
whole army passed in successive batches. It is time,
perhaps, that a common error should be exploded, into
which, however, it would be impossible for any atten-
tive reader of Herodotus to fall. No schoolboy believes now, as elderly men did when they were boys,
that the French are a nation of cowards. But it is
possible for careless readers of Greek history to
believe that the Persians were cowards; else, they
might say, how should they have been beaten by

so small a number of Greeks? And were they not
obliged to flog their soldiers into action? Perhaps
this was only a Greek version of the fact that corporal
punishment was an institution in their army. Amongst
the Greeks it was confined to slaves. The lash has not
prevented Russians and Austrians—not to mention
others—from fighting well. Perhaps the native Persians, especially those of noble birth, were personally
braver than the Greeks. But the Greeks had the immense advantage of discipline. In a disciplined army
every man has the eyes of his comrades on him, and if
fear is felt, it cannot act for very shame, and because
it is counteracted by mechanical obedience. Aristotle
assigns a special kind of courage to national militias,
which all Greek armies were, which he calls the political
courage, springing from the feeling of what is due from
the individual to the community. This may not be courage of the most romantic kind, but it appears to answer
its end perfectly; and Nelson thought it good enough
to appeal to in his famous watchword, still written round
the wheel of our war-ships—" England expects every
man to do his duty." This kind of courage culminated
in Leonidas. The Persian officers were even desperately
brave, and always led the charges in person, which
accounts for their great relative loss in battles. The
Greek officers took their chance with the rest, being
indistinguishable from the privates in the phalanx.
Again, the numbers of their armies were a positive disadvantage to the Persians; for most of their auxiliary
troops, when brought into contact with real soldiers,
were as sheep brought to the shambles. The Greeks
were also more efficiently armed. The Persian infantry
were archers, carrying also pikes and daggers, who (like

the English crossbow-man with his pavoise-bearer in
the fifteenth century) made a bulwark of their great
oblong wicker shields, as may be seen now in the Nim-
rud sculptures, and shot from behind them. But when
this bulwark was once forced, the Persians had no protection but their light armour against the strong pikes
of the Greeks. Our archers turned the scale of battle
against superior forces at Cressy and Poitiers, because
they were the only body which had at all the character
of regular troops.

The Persian officers had in some respects become
luxurious and effeminate even in the time of Darius,
riding in palanquins, keeping sumpter-camels, and so
forth; but they do not appear to have been worse than
our Anglo-Indians, who have never been reckoned defi-
cient in valour. The French *mousquetaires*, who fought
under Marshal Saxe, were as celebrated for their foppery
as their gallantry in the field. " Hold hard—the dandies
are coming !" was the word passed from one British
soldier to another, when their laced coats and three-
cornered hats came in sight.

There is no need to follow in detail all the pomp
and circumstance of the slow march of Xerxes into
Greece. The vast army crossed from Abydos to Sestos
by a double pontoon bridge; and Xerxes, like the
spoiled child of the harem, is said to have ordered the
Hellespont to be scourged, and chains to be thrown into
it, and branding-irons to be plunged into the hissing
water, because a storm had destroyed the work when
first attempted. He is also said to have cut in halves the
eldest son of a wealthy Lydian, who had made him an
offer of all his property, but requested that one of his
sons might be left behind; making his troops defile

between the severed portions, by way of raising their
enthusiasm. A similar story is told of Darius, which
appears, in his case, incredible. The great interest of
the expedition begins when it arrived where resistance
might be expected from the Greeks. The land-force
which marched round the coast was accompanied by
more than twelve hundred war-galleys, besides a multitude of other craft. The navy passed through a new-
made ship-canal, by which the voyage round the formidable headland of Athos was avoided. Our author
says the work was done in mere bravado, since the ships
might have been drawn across the narrow neck of land
with less labour and cost. It is remarkable, in the
cutting of this canal (a work of three years, the
traces of which are still distinctly visible), that all
the other nations were senseless enough to make its
sides perpendicular, which, from the continual landslips,
gave them double trouble ; while the Phœnicians alone
proved themselves as good "navvies" as navigators, by
making their cutting twice as broad at top as at bottom.

The news of the approach of this overwhelming
host struck the Greeks with consternation, and all the
northern tribes, including the Thebans, submitted to the
invader. The Athenians were alarmed by dark oracles
pointing apparently to their extermination, but containing one saving clause, that they might find safety
in their "wooden walls." They wisely interpreted
this to mean their ships. Their troublesome war with
the Æginetans proved now an advantage, as it had
forced them to make large additions to their navy, the
former poverty of which has been mentioned. Envoys
were sent for aid to Argos, Sicily, Corcyra, and Crete.
The Argives might be well excused for declining, as Cleo-

menes had just massacred six thousand out of their not probably more than ten thousand citizens. Gelon, the king of Syracuse, would have assisted, had not Sicily been just then invaded by a miscellaneous army of three hundred thousand men under the command of the Carthaginian Hamilcar, possibly induced, through the Phœnicians, to make this diversion in favour of Xerxes. Gelon had the good fortune to destroy this host in the decisive battle of Himera, on the same day as the Greek victory at Salamis. The Corcyræans temporised, with their historical selfishness ; the Cretans excused themselves on the faith of an oracle ; so the Greeks proper were left to face their terrible enemy alone, and even among them there were many craven spirits who took the side of the Persian.

Thessaly, through which the course of the invaders lay, is a basin of mountains, like Bohemia, cracked by the gorge of the Peneus, as Bohemia is by that of the Elbe. This basin was doubtless, as Herodotus says, once a lake, until it was tapped by some convulsion of nature. Xerxes thought flooding the country quite feasible, by damming up the outlet of the river : no such measure, however, was necessary. At first the Greeks had intended to make their stand there, in the Vale of Tempe, celebrated for its beauty. Overhung by plane-woods, the high cliffs are festooned with creepers, and diversified with underwood, approaching here and there so closely as to leave barely room for the road and river. But they gave up this position when they found that Thessaly could easily be entered by another road over the mountains. They drew back towards the isthmus : and Thessaly at once made terms with the Persian king.

It was now decided to make the first stand at the narrow pass of Thermopylæ (Hotwells-Gate), the key of Greece itself. The river Spercheius has since established a tract of alluvial deposit between the mountain and the sea, but the hot springs are still there, in pools of clear water, and the other features of the scene remain much as they were in the time of Herodotus. The pass leads along the shore from Thessaly to Locris. The Grecian fleet were to support the army in the narrow strait by Artemisium, on the head of Eubœa (Negropont). As the Persian host rolled on, it had increased like a snowball, imbibing the contingents of all the districts that submitted. But the elements were still against the invaders. A storm arose when their fleet was off Magnesia, attributed by the Athenians to the intervention of Boreas (the North Wind), who had married a daughter of their mythical king Erechtheus. At least four hundred galleys perished, and so much wealth was cast ashore that the wreckers on the coast became rich men ; and the Persians soon after lost fifteen ships more, which mistook the enemy's fleet for their own. Xerxes was himself with the land-force, which had now occupied the territory of Trachis, north of the pass of Thermopylæ. The little Greek army had posted itself behind an ancient wall, which barred the pass, and which they had repaired, at a spot where there was only room for a single chariot-road. The nucleus of the force (in all under 8000 of all arms) was three hundred thorough-bred Spartans, each attended by his seven Helots. They were all fathers of families, who had left sons at home to succeed them. At their head was Leonidas, now senior king of Sparta. This

small force was expected to be able to hold the pass
until the rest were disengaged; for the Spartans were
keeping a local feast, and the other Greeks were engaged at the great Olympian festival. Perhaps the very
extremity of the danger made the Greeks put their religious duties in the foreground; and, indeed, Leonidas
and his men went out as to an expected sacrifice. A
Persian scout reported to Xerxes that he found the
Spartans busy dressing their hair. In surprise the
king appealed for explanation to his refugee guest
Demaratus, the banished king of Sparta, whom he
had brought to Greece in his train. The Spartan
warned him that it betokened, on the part of his
countrymen, a resistance to the death. Usually careless of their dress, there was one occasion when they
polished their arms, combed their long hair and
wreathed it with flowers, and put on scarlet vests; it
was when they expected a battle which they might
not survive. Xerxes waited four days to see if they
would retire, and then ordered his Medes and Cissians
to bring them to him in chains. For a whole day
these made repeated attacks, and were as often repulsed with heavy loss. The Persian "Immortals"
were then launched at them, and fared no better.
These troops were so called because they were always
kept up to the exact number of ten thousand,* and represented the Imperial Guard. Often pretending flight,
so as to draw them on in loose pursuit, the Greeks
turned on their enemies and butchered them. One
would have thought that this affair in the front would
have made little impression on that dense host; but

---

* The forty members of the French Academy are so nick-
named for the same reason.

Xerxes is said to have leapt thrice from his throne as the wave of disturbance reached him, fearing for his whole army. On the third day a native guide came and told the king of a pass over the mountains, by which the Greeks might be taken in rear, and he selected Hydarnes, the commander of the Immortals, for this important service. The crest of this pass (the existence of which the Greeks had learned too late) was watched on their behalf by a thousand Phocians, who were warned by hearing the rustling of the dry leaves of the oak-wood, but thinking an attack on their own post was intended, retired to a more defensible position, and let Hydarnes pass on. The way in which the little band of heroes received the announcement that their position had been turned should be told in Herodotus's own words :—

"First, the soothsayer Megistias, as he inspected the sacrifices, warned them of the death which awaited them with the morrow's dawn. Then came some deserters, who told them of the march of the Persians round the hill. All this was while it was still night. Then, when the day had broken, their scouts came running down from the heights with the same news. Thereupon the Greeks took counsel, and their opinions were. divided : for some would not hear of quitting their post, while others advised to do so. Then they parted asunder, and some went off and dispersed each to their own cities, and some prepared to remain there with Leonidas. It is even said that Leonidas himself sent them away, anxious that they should not be slain ; but for himself and the Spartans who were there, it was not seemly, he said, for them to leave a post which they had once undertaken to keep."

Those who chose the nobler alternative, besides the Spartans and their Laconian subjects and Helot slaves, who could not help themselves, were seven hundred Thespians and four hundred Thebans—the latter, our author says, detained as hostages, but probably proscribed at home for refusing to submit, like the rest, to Xerxes. The struggle now could have but one issue. Xerxes ordered a general attack at daybreak, and Leonidas, in order to sell the lives of his men as dearly as possible, ordered them to advance from the defile itself, and attack in the open. The Persians perished in crowds—some driven into the sea, some trampled to death by their comrades, others urged forward by stripes only to fall on the deadly lances of the Greeks.

Dead weight, however, began to tell against the latter, when they had broken their spears in barbarian bodies, and had used their swords till they were weary. At last Leonidas fell, and over his body the struggle was renewed more furiously than ever.

> " The dead around him on that day
> In a semicircle lay."

In that swathe of corpses were found two brothers of Xerxes. Four times the Greeks repulsed the enemy, and at last bore off the body of their king. They had but short breathing-space. Their hour was come, when the fatal troops of Hydarnes came down the hills in their rear. The survivors drew back into the narrowest part of the pass, within the wall, and posted themselves on a hillock, where a stone lion afterwards marked the resting-place of Leonidas. So did the survivors of the Khyber Pass massacre in 1841 draw together for a last stand on the hillock at Gundamuck, whence a single officer escaped to Peshawur to tell that the British army was exterminated.

The four hundred Thebans saved themselves by a timely surrender; the remaining four thousand Greeks were buried in a hail-shower of missiles. Herodotus awards the palm of valour to a Spartan wit, who, when he was told that the Persian arrows would darken the air, said, "Then we shall have but a shadow-fight" (or sham-fight). Such a man would have appreciated the ghastly witticisms of the guillotine in the French Revolution. Xerxes, with an indecency towards the dead quite opposed to all Persian usage, had the head of Leonidas cut off, and fixed upon a pole.

The Greek combined fleet was commanded by the Spartan Eurybiades. The Spartans would only co-operate on condition that the command should be theirs, though they only furnished ten ships, while the Athenians mustered one hundred and twenty-seven. Spartan provincialism forms a strong contrast to the national patriotism of the little state of Platæa, which threw itself heart and soul into the cause of Greek independence. Though landsmen, the Platæans helped to man the Athenian fleet. They were afterwards rewarded by vile ingratitude from Sparta, and lukewarm friendship from Athens.

The whole naval strength counted two hundred and seventy-one three-banked galleys. The Persian disaster in the storm had now been balanced by a Greek disaster in the field ; and the barometer of Hellenic confidence fell again. There was even talk of leaving Eubœa to its fate, and retreating southwards. Themistocles, the Athenian commander, was a man who had raised himself to a foremost position from small beginnings, which may account for his understanding so well the use and power of money. If Mammon was one of his gods, he could make him his servant for good as well as for evil. The Eubœans, alarmed for their families and goods, besought the Spartan admiral not · to desert them; and finding him impracticable, applied to Themistocles—this time backing their prayers with a present of thirty talents. Themistocles knew Eurybiades better than they, and gave him five talents out of the thirty, as if they had come from himself, or from the treasury of the Athenians, and three more to Adeimantus the Corinthian, whose valour, among all the national commanders, seemed most strongly tempered with discretion. The rest of this secret-service money he kept for himself.

The Persians, in great fear lest the Greek fleet should escape them under cover of night, detached two hundred ships, with orders to sail round outside Eubœa, and back up the strait between the island and the mainland, and so block in the enemy.

The battle—or rather battles, for there were three —of Artemisium began by desultory and provocative attacks on the part of the Greeks, who, when they had brought the whole Persian fleet upon them, rolled theirs up like a hedgehog or porcupine, with the spines outside. They drew their sterns all together, and formed a circle with their sharp beaks turned every way. In the first *mêlée* thirty ships were taken from the Persians. The battle lasted through the midsummer evening, and then each fleet withdrew to its

moorings. The sea was like oil, and that ominous calm
reigned from which better sailors than the Greeks
would have foretold storm. At midnight it thundered
and lightened on Mount Pelion, the wind rose, and
the wrecks and bodies were drifted to the station of
the Persian fleet, and struck the crews with dismay.
But it fared worse with their detached division, which
was utterly destroyed on the rocks on the outer coast
of Euboea. Thus did the good wind Boreas still seem
to help his friends. A reinforcement of fifty-three
fresh Athenian galleys came up at daybreak, having
escaped the storm inside the island. The ancient war-
ships, even the great "five-bankers" of the Romans and
Carthaginians, could stand no more weather than a
river-steamer; while their great rounded Dutch-built
merchant-ships would ride out a moderate gale fairly.
On the afternoon of the second day the Greeks attacked
again, and sank some Cilician vessels. On the third
day about noon the Persians began the attack, while
the Greeks kept their station at Artemisium. There
was much fouling among the Persians from their closely-
packed vessels, but they fought well, and neither side
could claim much advantage. The Athenians gained
most distinction among the allies; and of the Athenians
Cleinias, son of Alcibiades, and father of him of that
name who afterwards was the representative Athenian
of the new school. He had manned and equipped his
trireme at his own expense. The Greeks remained
masters of the field—that is, of the scene of action,
with the bodies and wrecks; but as half the Athenian
fleet had been more or less damaged, they decided on
withdrawing southward, especially as they now heard of
the loss of Thermopylæ. Before he went, Themistocles

had inscriptions graven on the rocks by all the water-ing-places, exhorting the Ionian Greeks now in the service of Persia to desert. If this had no effect on those to whom they were addressed, it would at any rate make them objects of suspicion to the Persians. Then the Greeks sailed away—the Corinthians first, the Athenians, as became them, last.

While the Persian sailors and marines were wasting the north of Euboea, a herald came from Xerxes order-ing a day's leave ashore to be given, that the crews might view the field of Thermopylæ. On the Greek side were four thousand bodies in a heap, which the king pretended were all Spartans or Thespians; on his side lay about a thousand, scattered all over the field. The rest of the Persians had been carefully buried beforehand; but the trick deceived nobody.

The Persian army now advanced and ravaged Phocis, and on the farther frontier parted into two divisions, the larger entering the friendly territory of Boeotia, and making for Athens—the smaller proceeding to-wards Delphi. Xerxes was well instructed as to the wealth of Apollo's temple, and must have known by heart all the costly offerings that Crœsus had made. The Delphians in dismay consulted their oracle: the god replied that "he could protect his own." Just when the enemy reached the ascent to the temple, a thunderstorm burst forth, and great rocks came rolling down the steep of Parnassus. The Persians fled, and the Delphians, assisted apparently by two supernatural warriors, emerged from their hiding-places and slew the hindermost. The priests of Apollo were doubtless adepts in the machinery of the stage.

CHAPTER XI.

" The man of firm and righteous will,
　　No rabble, clamorous for the wrong,
No tyrant's brow, whose frown may kill,
　　Can shake the strength that makes him strong:
Not winds, that chafe the sea they sway,
　　Nor Jove's right hand, with lightning red:
Should Nature's pillared frame give way,
　　That wreck would strike one fearless head."
　　　　　　　　　　　—CONINGTON'S ' Horace.'

SUCH is the portrait of Themistocles, as drawn by Kaulbach of Munich, in his great cartoon of the battle of Salamis. He stands at ease on the deck of his galley, sacrificing to the gods while the battle is ending. We feel that he would be as composed and dignified, only somewhat sadder, if the ruin were coming on him instead of on the enemy. The very self-seeking of this remarkable man in the midst of the most exciting circumstances bears testimony to the admirable balance of his nature. He somewhat resembles Marlborough, of whom, for all his romantic courage, Macaulay too severely says, that in his youth he loved lucre more than wine or women, and in his middle age he loved lucre more than power or glory. But it

must be remembered that Themistocles was a Greek,
and the versatile Ulysses is the very type of a Greek
hero. It was not in the Greek character to vie with
Darius in his right royal disdain of petty advantage
and private revenge. The Greeks would have made far
better "hucksters" than that king, who was so called
by his nobles because he was a good financier. And
Themistocles was a first-rate example of the middle-
class burgher, as "the curled Alcibiades" was of the
"gilded youth" of a cultivated Greek republic. He
was Presence-of-mind incarnate. But he was honest
withal—with the honesty of a good Jew with whom
one might safely deposit millions, but who would not
fail to make every shilling breed. And he was a
patriot — one who would die for his country at any
moment, but was far too sensible to believe in her or
to trust her. The sequel of his life showed that he
was right. Themistocles, though not the highest type
of man, is perhaps the most perfect specimen of the
Greek on record.

The Athenians had hoped that the combined Greek
forces would make a stand in Bœotia, but in this they
were disappointed. The primary object of the Spartans
was to take care of themselves; their secondary object
to save Greece, that they might rule it. They wished
the Athenians out of their way, but they felt that if
the fire spread to them, it would be coming somewhat
close to their own home. Could they not sacrifice
Athens, and save the Athenians, who would then be
their obedient servants? So they withdrew their
land-forces behind the Isthmus of Corinth, which they
proceeded to fortify; while the combined fleet was in-

duced, by the entreaties of the Athenians, to anchor off the island of Salamis, to which most of the latter proceeded to transfer for safety their families and goods.

The Greeks had received reinforcements which made their fleet larger now than when it had fought at Artemisium. The Athenians now furnished one hundred and eighty of the three hundred and seventy-eight galleys. The Persian army entered Athens only to find an empty city—none had remained in it but some of the very poorest, or a few obstinate heads who saw in the palisade of the citadel the "wooden walls" of the oracle, and strengthened it with planks accordingly. The Persians encamped on the Areopagus (the Mars' Hill of St Paul), and shot lighted arrows at the barricade, which was soon in flames. But their storming-parties were foiled by a gallant defence, until a few soldiers scaled a place where no watch was kept, and were followed by others, who put the weak garrison to the sword. The temple of the goddess was plundered and burnt, and Xerxes sent a messenger home to Susa to announce that his vengeance was complete.

The sacrifice of Athens was unavoidable, yet it greatly affected the allies, who thought of withdrawing their fleet to the isthmus. But the Athenians felt that this step would almost certainly lead to its breaking up. There was a long war of words between Themistocles, Eurybiades, and Adeimantus. This last was insolent to the Athenian. "You have no country now," said he, "and therefore no vote." Themistocles replied, that with two hundred well-manned ships the Athenians would find a country wherever they chose to land. At last the threat that the Athenians would all emigrate to Italy, and give up the war, prevailed. And preparations were made for battle.

The time was naturally one which abounded with portents and prodigies, which were generally interpreted to the disadvantage of the enemy. It was the time of the year of the great procession in honour of Ceres and Bacchus from Eleusis to Athens. It could not be held now, in the presence of the enemy, but a chant was heard in the air, as from no mortal choir, and a column of dust was seen to rise, and spread into a heavy cloud which overshadowed the Persian armament. Some enthusiasts averred that they saw the heroes Ajax, Teucer, and Achilles, battling for their homesteads in Salamis and Ægina. Their images, at all events, were brought out to battle, for good-luck. The Spanish Carlists, when they appointed the image of Nostra Señora de los Dolores generalissimo of their forces, went a step further; and this was in our remembrance.

The Persian fleet had already lost six hundred and fifty ships, but Herodotus says that it had been reinforced to the original number by the contingents from the islands and some maritime states—an assertion which seems hardly probable. At Phalerum, the harbour of Athens, a council of war was held. The best head in the fleet of Xerxes was a woman's—Artemisia, queen of Halicarnassus. This Amazon of the sea seemed almost a match for that goddess of War and Wisdom whom the Athenians worshipped. She always appears a special favourite with her townsman Herodotus, who nevertheless is said to have found the tyranny of her family unendurable. She advised Xerxes to bide his time, and let the Greek confederacy fall to pieces from internal dissensions. But the

party of action prevailed; the land-forces marched on
the isthmus, where Cleombrotus, brother of Leonidas,
now commanded, and the fleet weighed anchor.

The Spartans and other Greeks within the Peninsula
had meanwhile been working night and day, throwing up a wall of defence across the isthmus. Their
panic communicated itself to the fleet, so that Themistocles was obliged at last to resort to a desperate stratagem. He sent to the Persian commanders secretly, to
tell them that he was a well-wisher of the king's, and
that the Greeks meditated flight. The Persians believed
it, and made such arrangements of their forces, under
cover of the night, as would effectually prevent the
escape of their enemies. The Greek council of captains
was still in fierce debate when the Athenian Aristides
arrived from Ægina, where he was undergoing ostracism
(he was said to have been banished because the people
were tired of hearing him called "the Just"), and said
that he had just succeeded in getting through the enemy,
who had completely surrounded the Greeks. All now
made up their minds for the inevitable fight, and
the commanders addressed the crews—Themistocles,
with the most powerful eloquence. But the enemy
attacked so fiercely that the Greeks backed water, till
Ameinias the Athenian, whose blood was hotter than
that of the rest, darted forward and engaged an enemy's
ship. The two became entangled, and others coming
up to their aid, the conflict became general. The Persians themselves fought better than at Artemisium,
although they became involved in the same inextri-
cable confusion, while the Greeks never allowed their
line to be broken. The very circumstance that the
Persians were under the eye of their king, who over-

looked the battle from a neighbouring promontory, told in one respect against them, since it caused those in the rear to press to the front, and thus get involved with their own retreating ships; so that a tangled ball of hulls, oars, and rigging, was formed, which the freely-moving Greeks could strike at and tear to pieces at their leisure.

The vanquished showed in some instances great gallantry. The liege lady of Herodotus, Queen Artemisia, distinguished herself as much in the fight as in the council, but in a way of questionable morality. Being hard pressed by an Athenian galley, she turned on one belonging to her own allies, and sank it. The Athenian thought he must have made a mistake, and sheered off, while the unsuspecting Xerxes admired the good service his fair ally seemed to be doing. "My men," said he, "fight like women, and my women like men." Such cool effrontery would have been unintelligible to a Persian. There was a petty king on board the galley which she had sunk; but drowned men tell no tales.

A brother of the king, Ariabignes, the admiral, perished, and a vast number of noble Persians. The Greeks whose ships were sunk mostly saved themselves by swimming, while the Persians lost more drowned than killed in action. The fugitives tried to reach Phalerum, but there were Æginetans outside, who swooped on them like falcons. The stage-coward of the battles of Artemisium and Salamis is the unfortunate Adeimantus, who is accused of attempted flight. Why was Herodotus, usually so impartial, so spiteful against him and the Corinthians? He may have relied on Athenian information, or perhaps some general impression of Greek half-heartedness must have come from Halicarnassian or Ionian sources. Æschylus,

in his magnificent tragedy of "The Persians," beside
which the prose of Herodotus is tame, speaks of
nothing but patriotic zeal, singing of pæans, and
joyous alacrity.   The hero of Waterloo is said to
have modestly observed to some ladies who compli-
mented him on a description of the battle, "I ought
to know all about it, for I was there myself."   So
Æschylus ought to be our best authority for the battle
of Salamis, as he was present himself, probably in the
ship of his brother Ameinias.   According to him, it was
the Persians who were caught in a trap by Themistocles : thinking the Greeks were in retreat, they had
made their arrangements for chase and not for action,
which rendered their discomfiture more easy; since
not only did those who came up break their fighting
order, but, as at Artemisium, they had detached a considerable squadron to block the entrance to the strait.
The poet describes the chase as lasting till midnight, in
the open sea, the Greeks destroying the helpless enemy
"like fishermen harpooning in a shoal of tunny-fish."
All the shore of Attica was strewn with wrecks.

"Slow sinks, more lovely ere his race be run,
  Behind Morea's hills the setting sun ;
  Not as in northern climes, obscurely bright,
  But one unclouded blaze of living light !
  O'er the hushed deep the yellow beam he throws,
  Gilds the green wave, that trembles as it glows.
  On old Ægina's rock, and Hydra's isle,
  The god of gladness sheds his parting smile ;
  O'er his own regions lingering, loves to shine,
  Though there his altars are no more divine.
  Descending fast, the mountain-shadows kiss
  Thy glorious gulf, unconquered Salamis !"*

* Byron—"The Corsair."

But never did the sun of Greece set on a scene so memorable, and so beautiful in one sense, in the midst of its terror, as on that autumn evening in the year 480 B.C. There was yet more to be done, but Greece and civilisation were safe.

The destruction of the grand fleet necessitated the retreat of the heterogeneous multitude which called itself the grand army, for it depended on the fleet for most of its supplies. But it was hoped that a picked force might still succeed, and Xerxes left behind 300,000 troops under the command of Mardonius, who went into winter quarters in Thessaly, when he started homewards with all possible speed. This flight may have had State reasons for it, like that of Napoleon from Russia, for the outlying provinces were always ready for insurrection; but, considering his character, the simple interpretation of his conduct appears the most probable, that he was thoroughly cowed. Themistocles wished to follow up the victory by hunting the fugitives from island to island, and then destroying the bridge of boats over the Hellespont. When he was overruled by Eurybiades, he gave out that he had changed his mind, and sent a faithful slave to find Xerxes, and tell him that, out of personal goodwill to his majesty, Themistocles had prevented the Greeks from destroying the bridge.

An unusually early winter, as in the Russian campaign of 1812, added to the sufferings of the retreat. According to the tragedian Æschylus, great numbers perished in attempting to cross the frozen Strymon, thus forestalling the Beresina disaster. The Hellespont bridge had been broken up, not by the Greeks but by a storm; but there was no difficulty in ferrying across the miserable remnant in boats. At Abydos they came on supplies, and many who had survived starvation on grass and tree-bark died of surfeit. One version of the account makes Xerxes leave his army on the Strymon, and take ship himself for Asia. A storm coming on, the ship was in such danger that the pilot declared that there was no chance of safety unless some of those on board would sacrifice themselves to lighten it, and appealed to the loyalty of the Persians, who accordingly leapt overboard. It is added that, on coming safely to land, the king presented the pilot with a golden crown for saving his own life, and then had him beheaded for causing the death of so many of his gallant servants. The latter part looks like the repetition of an anecdote of Cambyses; and indeed Herodotus scarcely believes the story, as he observes that the Persians might have been sent below, and the Phœnician crew sacrificed. It did not seem to strike him that sailors are of more use in a storm than the best soldiers, and the self-devoting loyalty of the Persians to their monarch's person is well known.

The Greeks passed an anxious winter, for Mardonius remained in Thessaly, making his preparations for action in the spring. Their allied fleet, a hundred and ten strong, was persuaded to come as far as Delos by an embassy from Asia (one of whom was an Herodotus, possibly a relative of our author), who represented that the Greek colonies there were ripe for revolt. They were, however, deterred for the present from proceeding farther; possibly because a Lacedæmonian, naturally a landsman, was first in command. Mardonius in the mean time spent the winter in con-

sulting oracles, the answers of which do not seem to
have been particularly encouraging, as he afterwards
resorted to the more statesmanlike measure of endeavouring to detach the Athenians from the Greek alliance. For this mission he selected Alexander, the son
of Amyntas, prince of Macedon. The Spartans, hearing of it, sent ambassadors on their part to beseech
them not to desert the cause of Greece. The Athenians, with something of a lofty contempt, bade them
have no fear, and told Alexander that they would
carry on the war with the destroyers of their city and
temples " so long as the sun held its course in heaven"
—and warned him, as he valued his safety, never again
to bring them a like proposal. They were terribly in
earnest ; for when one Lycidas, a fellow-townsman,
counselled submission on another occasion, they stoned
him to death.

CHAPTER XII.

PLATÆA AND MYCALE.

" A day of onsets of despair !
Dashed on every rocky square,
Their surging charges foamed themselves away.
Last the Prussian trumpet blew;
Through the long-tormented air
Heaven flashed a sudden jubilant ray,
And down we swept, and charged, and overthrew."
—TENNYSON : " Ode on the Death
of the Duke of Wellington."

THE concluding act of the great historical drama opens
with the spring of B.C. 479. Mardonius has come
south from Thessaly, and is gleaning in Athens whatever the spoiler, Xerxes, had left. The Athenians are
again in their island-asylum of Salamis. The Spartans
are marching on the Isthmus of Corinth, under the
command of Pausanias, who had succeeded his father
Cleombrotus in the regency and the guardianship
of the young son of Leonidas, who did not live to
reign. After a demonstration towards Megara,
where he hoped to cut off the advanced-guard
of the allies, Mardonius proceeded into the Theban
territory, where he constructed a vast fortified camp
on the bank of the river Asopus. A general ad-

vance was now made by the Peloponnesians from
the isthmus to Eleusis, where they were joined by the
Athenian contingent from Salamis. When they had
ascertained where the Persians were, they set themselves in array along the highlands of Cithæron. As
they seemed indisposed to come down into the plain,
Mardonius sent his cavalry to feel their position, under
the command of Masistius.

This Murat of the Persian army was a handsome giant, who rode a white Nisæan charger, whose
accoutrements, as well as those of his rider, glit-
tered with gold. So rode Charles of Burgundy at
Granson or at Morat. In the present day such cos-
tume is scarcely to be seen further west than India,
and some tall Rajah, full dressed for the Governor-
General's durbar, would give a good idea of how Masistius looked at the head of his cuirassiers. These
galloped up to the Greek infantry in troops, hurling
their javelins, and calling them " women " because they
did not come on. The Megarians were in the most
exposed place. Being hard pressed, they sent to
Pausanias for succour. When he called for volunteers,
the Athenians promptly offered, and three hundred
picked men, supported by archers, moved up. The
charges continued without cessation, Masistius leading
with the utmost gallantry, and presenting a conspicu-.
ous mark to the bowmen. At last an arrow pierced
the side of his charger. He reared back from the
agony of the wound, and threw his rider, who now
lay at the mercy of his enemies, stunned by his
fall, and, like the knights of the middle ages, helpless from the weight of his panoply. His vest
of Tyrian crimson was pierced with spear-points, but

still he lived, for under it he wore a shirt of golden
mail. At last a hand more dexterous than the rest
pierced his brain through one of the eye-holes of his
visor, for he was too proud to ask for quarter. Amongst
his own followers, as they charged and wheeled about,
no one knew that he was dead, and they might even
have ridden over the body of their unconscious commander, as the Prussian cavalry did over Blucher when
he lay under his dead horse at Ligny. But when they
retired he was immediately missed, for there was no
one to give the word of command. All that they could
now do for him was to recover his body, and with this
object the squadrons united and made a combined onset.
To meet this, the Athenians called up other Greek
troops to their assistance. While they were coming,
a fierce struggle took place for the body, which the
Athenians were obliged to leave till their reinforcements
joined them. But as it could not be easily removed
by cavalry, it ultimately remained in possession of
the Greeks. Many Persian knights shared the fate of
their commander, so that the rest of the troopers were
obliged to ride back to Mardonius with the news of
their misfortune. The death of Masistius was considered such a blow that it was bewailed by the whole
army, corps after corps taking up the dole of their
Adonis, till it resounded through all Bœotia, and horses
and men were ordered to be shorn and shaven as a
sign of public mourning; for Masistius, next to Mardonius, was considered the greatest man in the army. To
the Greeks his fall was a matter of equal rejoicing, and
the handsome corpse was carried along the lines to
raise the spirits of the soldiers. Their fear of cavalry
was now wearing off, and a general forward movement

was made towards the plain of Platæa, where water
was more abundant. They took up a new position near the Gargaphian Fountain (the modern Ver-
gantiani). Here a hot debate arose between the
Tegeans and Athenians, each demanding the honour
of occupying the left wing (the Spartans always claimed
the right), which was decided, chiefly on mythological
grounds, in favour of the Athenians. The army was
thus marshalled : on the right were five thousand
heavy-armed Spartans, with thirty-five thousand light-
armed Helots, and of other Laconians five thousand ;
then the Tegeans, then the other Greek contingents, till
on the extreme left six hundred Platæans stood by the
side of eight thousand Athenians under Aristides. The
decision of Greek battles mainly rested on the heavy-
armed infantry. Each man of these was generally attended by his military servant, and looked upon himself
as an officer and a gentleman. The Athenian contingent probably represented all who were not engaged on
board the fleet. The remnant of the Thespians—whose
city as well as Platæa had been sacked—eighteen hundred in number, were also there, but now too much
impoverished to serve as heavy-armed. The sum total
of the army was one hundred and ten thousand men,
being less than one to three to the army of the king.

Mardonius honoured the Spartans by confronting
them with his best troops, the Persians ; he posted
his Medes, Bactrians, Indians, and Sacæ opposite the
other Greeks, and threatened the Athenians with his
Greek and Macedonian allies. Besides his three hundred thousand, he had a number of small contingents,
such as marines from the fleet, and perhaps fifty thousand Greek auxiliaries. It was not the custom for

any army to engage until the omens had been pronounced favourable ; and the soothsayers on both sides
constantly reported that they were favourable for defence, but not for attack.   After the two armies had
thus watched each other for eight days, Mardonius was
advised to occupy the passes of Cithæron, as the Greeks
were constantly being reinforced from that quarter, and
accordingly despatched cavalry to a pass leading to
Platæa, called "Three Heads" by the Bœotians, and
"Oakheads" by the Athenians (the Greek words
sounding much the same).   This foray resulted in
destroying a military train of five hundred sumpter
animals, which was making its way to the Greek army.
The two next days were passed in demonstrations of
cavalry up to the Asopus, which ran between the
armies, the Theban horse showing great alacrity in
annoying their Hellenic brethren, but leaving the serious
fighting to the Persians.   On the eleventh day Mardonius, tired of inaction, held a council of war, the
result of which was that he ordered an attack on the
next day, in spite of the still unfavourable auspices.

In the dead of night, as the armies lay in position,
the Athenian sentries were accosted by a solitary horse-
man who asked to speak to their commanders.   When
they came to the front, he told them that the omens
had till now restrained Mardonius, but that yesterday
he had "bid the omens farewell," and intended to
fight on the morrow.   He added, that he hoped that
his present service would not be forgotten ; he was of
Greek origin, and a secret friend of the Greeks:
his name was Alexander, the son of Amyntas of
Macedonia.   As soon as the message had been reported
to Pausanias, he, with a scarcely Spartan spirit,

wished the Athenians to change places with him, as, from their experience at Marathon, they knew the Persian manner of fighting better. And this manœuvre, dangerous as it was to attempt in the face of the enemy, would have been executed, had not Mardonius discovered it, and made a corresponding disposition of his own army. He then sent a herald to reproach the Spartans, and challenge them to fight man for man, with or without the rest of the combatants, as they pleased. As no answer was given, his cavalry were launched *en masse* against the Greek army. The mounted archers caused them great annoyance, and destroyed the Gargaphian well, from which their water supply was drawn. The supplies from the rear having been cut off, the Greeks determined on a westward movement towards the city of Platæa, where they would be within reach of water. Half the army were to carry out this movement in the night, while the other half were to fall back on Cithæron, to protect their line of communication with their base behind the isthmus. The first division had suffered so much during the day, that in their joy at the respite they retired too far, and never halted till they reached the precincts of a temple of Juno, close to Platæa itself. Pausanias himself was following, but he was kept back by the insubordination of a sturdy colonel named Amompharetus, who objected to any strategic movements which looked like running away. At length he was left to follow or not, as he pleased, while the rest of the Spartans defiled along the safe and hilly ground, the Athenians striking across the exposed plain. Mardonius had now some reason to despise his enemy, and he ordered all his cavalry to charge, and the infantry to advance at quick march, crossing the Asopus. The Athenians were hidden from him by a series of knolls, but he pressed hard on the steps of the Lacedæmonians and Tegeans. Fortune sometimes favours the timid as well as the brave. Seeing Mardonius apparently pursuing the enemy, the rest of his army at once broke their ranks and followed in disorder, each man eager to be in at the death of the quarry which his commander was hunting down. Pausanias had already sent a mounted orderly to the Athenians to beg that they would come to his assistance, or at least send their archers, as he was sorely vexed by the cavalry. They could not comply, as they wanted all their strength to repulse a general attack which was just then being made on them by the king's Greeks. Pausanias halted his line; but still the sacrifices were unpropitious. From behind the Persian breastwork of shields came a rain of arrows, and the breastwork itself seemed impregnable. The Lacedæmonians and Tegeans were falling fast. At last Pausanias espied at no great distance the temple of Juno, and offered up a prayer to the goddess. The omens at once changed, as by magic. The Tegeans dashed at the enemy's fence of shields. The Spartans followed, and the battle was won. The Persians fought like bull-dogs, singly or in knots, though their long dress, says the chronicler, was terribly in the way. They wrenched away or snapt asunder the long Greek lances, and made play with their hangers. Mardonius, conspicuous on a white horse, like Ney at Waterloo, was the "bravest of the brave." But at last a cry rose that Mardonius was down, and at that cry the Persians wavered, and fled in wild

disorder to the great stockade which had been built
to protect their camp. But Artabazus, who had now
come up, had kept his forty thousand men in hand
when he saw the scramble of the attack; and when
he saw the repulse, he made no attempt to save the
day, but faced about and at once began an orderly
retreat on the Hellespont. Some of the Greeks who
had joined the Persian king fought desperately in
their miserable cause. Three hundred noble Thebans
are said to have fallen in the front of the battle.
This may have been the "Sacred Band" which fought
under Epaminondas in later history, and which consisted of friends sworn to live and die together. These
Thebans fought indeed "with halters round their
necks:" for after the victory, Pausanias insisted on
the surrender of the chiefs of the late movement,
and executed them all. When the Greeks who had
made the mistake of retreating too far turned back
in disorder to get their share of the glory, poetical
justice overtook them in the shape of a charge of
the Persian and Theban cavalry, which stung them
with the energy of a doomed swarm of wasps. They
lost six hundred men, and were scattered to the heights
of Cithæron. All was not yet over. A new battle
began at the Persian camp, which vigorously repelled
the onslaughts of the Spartans and their allies. It
was not till the Athenians came up (who understood
" wall-fighting," says Herodotus) that the day could be
spoken of as finally decided. They managed to break
or upset the "abattis," and the Tegeans again led
the forlorn hope through it or over it. Then began
the slaughter. Only three thousand were left alive
of the whole Persian army. This seems incredible,

especially in connection with the small number of the allies who fell in the action, as given by Herodotus. But the vanquished were possibly impounded in their fortified camp, like the wretched Mamelukes whom Mehemet Ali destroyed in the court of a fortress.

The plunder was immense. The tent of Mardonius, with all the royal plate which the king had left him, his manger of bronze, gold and silver in all shapes, splendidly inlaid arms, vestments, horses, camels, beautiful women, became the dangerous prize of the needy Peloponnesians, who, to avert Nemesis, offered a tithe of all to the gods. Pausanias buried with due honours the body of the brave Mardonius, though he was strongly urged by an Æginetan of high rank to remember how that of Leonidas had been treated by Xerxes. " Would you have me humble my country in the dust, now that I have just raised her ? " was the Spartan's answer. And he bid the proposer be thankful that he answered him only in words.

It seems to have been the invidious custom in all Greek battles to assign to one or two men the prize of valour, and our author always gives their names. The bravest of all was adjudged to be the Spartan Aristodemus, sole survivor of the glorious three hundred of Thermopylæ. He could not bear his life, and now lost it purposely ; therefore he was refused the usual honours. Sophanes was proclaimed the bravest of the Athenians : he was in fact so brave that (perhaps adopting an idea from his experience afloat) he wore an anchor and chain, by which he moored himself to his post in action.* It is

* So the wounded at the battle of Clontarf, in Ireland, are said to have got themselves tied to stakes.

a pity to lose our faith in so quaint an expedient ; but there was another version of the story, says our honest chronicler, that he bore an anchor as the device on his shield. The prudent Artabazus reached Byzantium safely, though he was roughly handled on the road by the Thracians and Macedonians, the latter of whom had been from the first favourable to the Greeks.

This "crowning mercy" of Platæa, as Cromwell would have called it, was supplemented by a brilliant action which took place on the same day at Mycalè, on the coast of Ionia.

When the season for navigation had come, the Greek fleet under Leotychides, which had remained at Delos, pushed across to Samos, but the prey they had expected to find there had flown. The Persian fleet had placed itself under the protection of a land force of sixty thousand men under Tigranes, appointed by Xerxes governor of Ionia, and was drawn up on shore at Mycalè, protected by a rampart and palisade. The Greeks came provided with gangway boards, and all other appliances for naval action. But the Persians were morally sea-sick, therefore Leotychides disembarked his troops at his leisure. A mysterious rumour of a great victory in Bœotia, ascribed to some divine messenger, but possibly brought as a telegram by fire-signals, put the Greeks in heart. It was afternoon, and the field of Platæa had been fought in the morning. The Athenians were already engaged, when the Lacedæmonians came up, having to make a circuit by a rugged way intersected with ravines. As at Platæa, the Persians fought well as long as their rampart of bucklers stood upright : even when it gave way, they broke up into clusters, which fought like wild boars at bay.

The onset of the Athenians was the more furious that they feared to have their laurels snatched from them by their friends.   They drove the Persians into their camp, and, more fortunate than their brethren at Platæa, entered it pell - mell with the flying enemy. The barbarian auxiliaries fled where they could, but the Persians themselves still held out desperately, until the Lacedæmonians came up and completed the defeat.   Tigranes and Mardontes died as became Persian officers, fighting gallantly to the last.   The Milesians in the Persian service, who had been posted to guard the passes of the mountain, turned on the fugitives and cut them up; for revolt became general among the Ionian Greeks as soon as the battle was over, and Samos, Chios, Lesbos, and other islands, joined the confederacy for reprisals against Persia.

The Greek fleet now sailed to the Hellespont, where they found the bridge of boats destroyed.   Then Leotychides went home with his Spartans, but the Athenians stayed and besieged Sestos, which held out till the autumn, when it was taken by famine.   There had been a serious debate whether it would not be better to remove the Ionian colonists altogether, and settle them in Greece, than leave them to the future tender mercies of Persia.   But the question was settled by the Athenians taking their Asiatic colonies into close league and alliance.

In those two memorable years, which end the narrative of Herodotus, Europe had established its preponderance over Asia for ever.   The last tableau of his great epic drama is almost lost in its blaze of glory, and it is time that the curtain should fall.   It is true that Herodotus hardly recognises this, and tries to amuse his readers for some time longer with the not very edifying court-scandal of Susa. Xerxes had infinite trouble with the ladies of his court. The fierce and jealous sultana Amestris, who treated her rival with such fiendish cruelty, may be the Vashti of the Book of Esther, as Ahasuerus is supposed to be the Scriptural form of her husband's name. Nemesis was fully satisfied when Xerxes himself fell a victim to a palace intrigue; but this is not mentioned by Herodotus, nor that a statue of that dread Power was placed on the spot where he had been a spectator of the destruction of his fleet.

CHAPTER XIII.

CONCLUDING REMARKS.

IT has thus been attempted to give, in a succinct form, the general drift and character of the great work of Herodotus. In the original, his liquid and pellucid Ionian dialect constitutes one of the greatest charms of his style. In simple perspicuity he forms a remarkable contrast to the terse and gnarled Thucydides, who propounds so many puzzles to the classical scholar. But no ancient author is so profitable to read in a good translation. A good translation is like a good photograph, giving distinctive traits, and light and shade, but no life or colour. Our attempt is a coloured sketch on a small scale, and not a photograph, of a great book.

Herodotus may be considered, according to the standard of his time, as a decidedly veracious historian. And his veracity is of the kind that wears well. It is impossible to refuse to credit him with general impartiality; and if he erred at all, the modern reader will readily pardon his excessive sympathy with the Athenians. Yet he does full justice to the gallantry, generosity, and other high qualities of the Persians. He was born, we must remember, a Persian subject,—for Halicarnassus did not recover its independence until he had grown up to manhood—and he could speak from experience of the masters of Ionia, that their rule was, on the whole, just and equal. His own town, indeed, had met with exceptional kindness from her liege lords. Hence he has none of the usual Greek contempt of and antipathy to "barbarians," or people speaking an unknown tongue, which is a *primâ facie* reason for dislike with the vulgar of all nations. His great merit is that of Homer and Shakespeare, a broad catholicity of sentiment in observing and estimating character. He has the strongest sympathy with heroism whenever displayed, an exquisite feeling for humorous situations, and, as naturally connected with humour, intense pathos when the subject admits of it. He has the head of a sage, the heart of a mother, and the simple apprehension of a child. And if his style is redundant with a sort of Biblical reiteration, it is always clear and luminous. There can never be any mistake about his meaning, as long as no corruption has crept into his text, which, when it happens, is the fault of his transcribers, and not his own. His ethical portraits are above all invaluable, and, however fabulous the circumstances with which they are connected, must have been true to the life, from their evidently undesigned consistency. The benignant and vain Crœsus, the ambitious Cyrus, the truculent Cambyses, the chivalrous yet calculating Darius, the wild Cleomenes, the wise and wary Themistocles, the frantic Xerxes—the very type of the infatuation by which the divine vengeance wrought—these, and a host of other portraits of living men, can only be compared in their verisimilitude with the immortal creations of Shakespeare.

Not a few pleasant anecdotes—mythical, ethical,

social, and historical—as well as nearly all the minor affluents of the main stream of narrative, have been passed over or barely glanced at, for want of space. Some indelicacies have been softened in stories too good to omit, but this process leaves their spirit unchanged. For our author is always antique and always natural. When he errs against refinement, it is in a sort of infantine naughtiness — not with the perverse intention of a modern writer. Indeed, his high moral principle cannot fail to strike even a careless reader. His blood plainly boils at injustice or cruelty ; and whatever superstition he may have inherited with his religious creed, he has an intense faith in an overruling Providence, which, spite of some anomalies which puzzle him, as they have done the wisest in all ages, does on the whole ordain that "the righteous shall be recompensed in the earth—much more the wicked and the sinner."

END OF HERODOTUS.

PRINTED BY WILLIAM BLACKWOOD AND SONS, EDINBURGH.

Lightning Source UK Ltd.
Milton Keynes UK
UKHW020642090223
416652UK00001B/120